THE WORLD OF RUTH DRAPER

The World of Ruth Draper

A Portrait *of an* Actress

Dorothy Warren

With a Foreword by Helen Hayes

Southern Illinois University Press
Carbondale and Edwardsville

Copyright © 1999 by Dorothy Warren, Trustee of the Dorothy
    Warren Living Trust
Printed in the United States of America
02 01 00 99 4 3 2 1

Frontispiece: The Draper family, New York, 1897. *Standing from left to right:*
Alice, George, Charles, William, Dorothea. *Seated:* Ruth, Mrs. Draper, Paul,
Dr. Draper, Martha.

Library of Congress Cataloging-in-Publication Data
Warren, Dorothy, 1905–
    The world of Ruth Draper : a portrait of an actress / Dorothy Warren ; with
a foreword by Helen Hayes.
        p. cm.
    Includes index.
    1. Ruth Draper, 1884–1956. 2. Actors—United States Biography. I. Title.
    PN2287.D549W37 1999
    792'.028'092—dc21
    [B]   99-26765
    ISBN 0-8093-2162-9 (cl. : alk. paper)   CIP

The paper used in this publication meets the minimum requirements of
American National Standard for Information Sciences—Permanence of Paper
for Printed Library Materials, ANSI Z39.48-1984. ∞

Dedicated to
the family and friends of
Ruth Draper
who contributed so significantly to
this telling of her story

Contents

Illustrations

The Draper family, New York, 1897 *Frontispiece*

Following page 54

Vive la France—1940, 1946

Ruth Draper with Theater in der Josefstadt poster, June 1956

Charcoal drawing of Ruth Draper by John Singer Sargent, 1913

Eunice Dana Brannan (Aunt Nin), Ruth holding baby Diana, and Mrs. Draper, July 1914

Ruth Draper at a costume ball, 1922

Lauro de Bosis, Portonovo, 1920

Lauro de Bosis with his sister Elena Vivante, Leone Vivante, and their first child, Paolo, October 1921

Living room of Ruth Draper's apartment at 66 East 79th Street, c. 1938

Ruth Draper at Islesboro with Salvemini and Anne Draper, c. 1943

Ruth Draper at Islesboro with seven small English visitors and two friends, c. 1943

Ruth Draper sails her twelve-foot boat, the *Flickamaroo*

Raimund Sanders Draper, c. 1942

Ruth Draper and her nephew Paul Draper, 1951

Ruth Draper, c. 1950

Ruth Draper onstage in *Opening a Bazaar*

Ruth Draper offstage opens *The Mudlark*, June 11, 1951

Ruth Draper as the Grandmother in *Three Generations in a Court of Domestic Relations*

Ruth Draper as Mrs. Clifford, c. 1950

Illustrations

Foreword

IT IS GOOD TO HAVE RUTH DRAPER back with us with her rich understanding of humanity and the world around her. How she could make an audience glow with recognition. I was one of her many friends. She had a gift for making friends because of her keen interest in people, naturally since we were the subjects of her art.

Too bad she came before the video tape, but this well-researched book will in a fashion make up for our loss.

Read and enjoy.

Helen Hayes
August 9, 1991

Preface

ON THE AFTERNOON OF JANUARY 16, 1923—I had just turned seventeen—my mother took me to the Broadhurst Theatre in New York to see Ruth Draper in a performance of six of her monologues, which she called "character sketches," plus her recently introduced *Five Imaginary Folk Songs*.

I was fascinated. This was pure magic! Over the next thirty-three years, I saw Ruth Draper perform thirty-seven times. During her long runs at the Comedy Theatre in 1929 and 1930, I systematically tried to see in performance each one of her personifications.

In another context, I had come to know her manager, Helen Arthur, and her stage manager, Emeline Roche. In due time I was invited backstage. I was very careful to stay out of the way and become nearly invisible. Occasionally I was invited to Miss Draper's dressing room for a chat during intermission; I was fascinated by the interplay of visitors after the show. More and more frequently, because I lived nearby, I took her home in a taxi—sometimes she never spoke all the way up through Central Park to 79th Street. Very shortly, Miss Draper told the guard at the stage door, "Miss Warren may come in the stage door whenever she wishes," and said to me, "Dorothy Warren, I'll not have you buying any more tickets to see me!"

Twenty-some years after this—in the 1950s—I again encountered her sister, Dorothea Draper (now Mrs. Henry James III), on some of whose charitable committees I had served during my debutante years, and also Aileen Tone, who had known me as a small child. Now there was *our* bond of all being graduates of Miss Spence's School. I went often to tea with each of them. It was Aileen Tone, in 1965, who spoke with me about Ruth Draper's letters and urged me to take on their editing. With a demanding full-time career and many pro bono obligations, I could not then think seriously about this task, although I did discuss the possibility with Alice Draper Carter. The last thing Aileen Tone said to me before her death in 1969 was, "Promise me that you will edit Ruth's letters—*you* are the person to write about her."

By the time I could give my full attention to Ruth Draper, who had died in 1956, Alice Draper also had died, in 1970, and Dorothea in 1960, and Harriet Marple was too ill to talk with me. I reached William Draper Carter, Alice's son, who came to tea and enthusiastically endorsed the plan, promising full cooperation. In the event, it was, for many years, something less than full. "Aunt Ruth" had not appointed a literary executor, and Bill's understanding of copyright was sketchy indeed. His sister, Ruthie Carter, more business-minded than her academic brother, was, not unreasonably, wary of me, a stranger in their midst.

It took a lawyer to discover and research five wills, over two generations—and to determine the fifteen legal heirs whose conveying of common law copyright had to be obtained before I was in the clear. In 1979, Scribner's published *The Letters of Ruth Draper*. That, I thought, was that.

Involved in another project, I had no thought of biography until 1984, by which time the boxes had begun to come down from top shelves: Ruthie Carter found a large dress box packed with every letter "Aunt Ruth" had ever written to Alice Carter, as well as a carton of letters and papers Alice had cleared out of Dorothea's desk and *her* top shelf. She sent me off in a taxi with two full cartons and a shopping bag—all loaded. It was a gold mine! I took fire, again! Bill sent me the "Mudie letters" about Lauro de Bosis's family, and Neville Rogers sent me copies of all the letters he had from Ruth—and was, himself, a mine of information about de Bosis. So began what was then called "Magic Carpet." Bill was delighted: "You are now the expert and can write what you want." And so I have.

Working chronologically, I came to 1928 and enter Lauro de Bosis. There was such a variety of—mostly conflicting—reports, writings, claims, and gossip about him and about his anti-Fascist activities that it was essential to research and reconstruct his entire story before proceeding. I thought it might take two months. I talked with cousins and nephews in this country, his sister in Italy, spoke at length with his English flying instructor, now living in California, and a wide-ranging group of friends and acquaintances. Gradually, the man—his personality and mind-set—emerged. It took two years and resulted in a separate manuscript concerned only with de Bosis's arrival at martyrdom. After living so intensely into his mind, it took months to clear mine before I could proceed with "Magic Carpet."

Then Ruthie Carter died, leaving a large manila envelope addressed "For Dorothy Warren," which contained all that she had withheld—Ruth Draper's will (which only my lawyer had seen), detailed instructions to her executor, and all the letters written to the family at the time of Ruth's death. Six months later, Bill died. His widow phoned me: "I have two cartons of Bill's Aunt Ruth papers and a box full of family photographs. Come and get what you want." I took the lot.

Closest to Ruth Draper in the next generation, besides Bill Carter, were Penelope Draper Buchanan and Paul Draper. All were forthcoming and frank, as was Elisabeth Draper, Dr. George's widow. Friends and acquaintances, so *many* of them (even those who disliked her for some thoughtless social snub), were eager to talk. Doors flew open at the mere mention of Ruth Draper's name. "Magic Carpet," now called *The World of Ruth Draper*, puts much of this on the record.

This is a formidable responsibility that has nearly overwhelmed my life, much as it has enlarged and broadened it. Ruth, ever the instructor, would be delighted.

The Letters are what Ruth Draper thought. *The World of Ruth Draper* fills in her life and tells what the rest of us understood about her. Read it carefully and may you, too, be rewarded, for she was like no other.

Acknowledgments

THE NEXT GENERATION OF THE DRAPER family, William Draper Carter, Ruth Dana Carter, Penelope Draper Buchanan, Paul N. S. Draper, his wife Heidi and his daughters, Susan, Pamela, and Kate, as well as Sanders Draper's daughter, Anne Draper, have been extraordinarily honest and cooperative. George Draper's widow, Elisabeth Carrington Frank Draper, twenty years his junior, has provided insights and the objective viewpoint of one "in but not of" the family. All descriptions of character or personality traits have been reviewed by the senior nieces and nephews, who often supplied the key to this biographer's understanding; they were close to their Aunt Ruth and were her special concern. It has been a reassuring experience to write with such open and enthusiastic encouragement.

Thanks also to Dorothea and Alice, Ruth Draper's sisters, and her close friends Aileen Tone (who urged me to undertake this work), Laura Chanler White, Alice Burnham Boit, Helen Salmond, and Joyce Grenfell, as well as Gertrude Schirmer Fay, Mrs. Henry Parish II, who was her goddaughter, and G. Herman Kinnicutt. Interviews by the author, as noted in *The Letters of Ruth Draper*, remain an ongoing obligation and basic to all ensuing research. At the mere mention of Ruth Draper's name, all doors flew open, thus providing an astonishing breadth of perspective.

Particular gratitude of the Draper family as well as of the author went to Helen Hayes for her warm appreciation of Ruth Draper.

In view of the openness of the conversations noted, it can confidently be stated that however intimately the personal characteristics and family relationships may be described, there is no assumption or conjecture, all conclusions having been carefully examined and weighed in the balance. Nearly twenty years has been spent in the research and study of Ruth Draper's life and that of Lauro de Bosis.

I gratefully acknowledge the following sources for permission to reprint selected materials: letter of Cornelia Conger (December 1956) quoted by permission of her son; letter of Alice Shurtleff quoted by permission of her son, John L. Shurtleff; letter by Janet Dana Longcope quoted by permission of Mary Lee Johansen; letter to Ruth Draper from Bernard Berenson quoted by permission of the Berenson Archive—Villa I Tatti, Harvard University Center for Italian Renaissance Studies, Florence; letters of Lauro de Bosis to Ruth Draper, and one to his mother, the source of phrases quoted throughout the retelling of events from April 1, 1928, through October 3, 1931, portions of which have been published in English in *Italy To-Day* (Nos. 11 and 12, November–December 1931) by Friends of Italian Freedom (Henderson's, London) and in Italian in Lauro de Bosis's *La storia della*

Acknowledgments

mia morte e ultima scritti, edited by Gaetano Salvemini and copyright by Francesco De Silva, 1948, Turin, quoted by permission of Arturo Vivante.

Grateful acknowledgment is made also for permission to quote a poem by Edith Wharton and note dated December 17, 1931, reprinted by permission of the Estate of Edith Wharton and the Watkins/Loomis Agency, as well as to the George La Piana Papers, bMS 104/30 (20) Andover-Harvard Theological Library of Harvard Divinity School, Cambridge, MA for permission to quote from four letters to George La Piana by Ruth Draper; to Benedetta Origo for permission to quote letters by members of the de Bosis family to Ruth Draper, as published in *A Need to Testify* by Iris Origo; to the late Joyce Grenfell for permission to quote conversations and correspondence as well as from *Joyce Grenfell Requests the Pleasure;* to Arturo Vivante for permission to quote from the letters of Lilian de Bosis to Ruth Draper, from Lauro de Bosis's poem, "Ciascun mattino sugli azzurri monti . . . ," and from the text of a BBC broadcast made on October 1, 1941, by Elena de Bosis Vivante, commemorating the tenth anniversary of the flight of Lauro de Bosis. Also thanks to Artemis Cooper for permission to quote a letter of Lady Diana Cooper from *A Durable Fire* as well as to Columbia University for permission to quote from a letter written by Ruth Draper to Marie Mattingly Meloney from the Marie Mattingly Meloney Papers, Rare Book and Manuscript Library, Columbia University.

Special thanks are due to my good friends who have put up with me these many months, supported and cosseted me through the shifting winds of this exacting concentration, to Patricia Norcia for consultation in the analysis of Ruth Draper's monologues and craft, and to David Kaplan, who, in the midst of his own far-flung work, has taken time to consult and given of his specialized knowledge and sensibility in the construction of this biography, so near to theatre itself.

Chronology

1922	June: Recites for Sarah Bernhardt.
	November: Performs in Madrid and before King Alfonzo and the royal family.
	December 19: Recites for Eleanora Duse.
1923	October 23: Produces "The Wedding Bells."
1925	February 15: Death of brother, Paul Draper.
	May 7: Recites at American embassy in Brussels before King and Queen of the Belgians and Cardinal Mercier.
	May–June: Travels to Greece.
1926	January 5: Death of half-brother, William K. Draper.
	June 18: Command performance at Windsor Castle.
1927	August 15: Dines with Max Reinhardt at Schloss Leopoldskron and recites.
1928	January: Is presented by Max Reinhardt in Berlin.
	February: Is presented by Max Reinhardt in Vienna, Munich, and Frankfort.
	March 14: Performs for Mussolini and meets Lauro de Bosis in Rome.
	May 23: Is presented at Court of St. James.
1929	January–April: Performs at Comedy Theatre, New York, for eighteen-week season.
	June–July: Performs in Poland. Travels to Russia.
	August: Visits de Bosis family in Ancona.
1930	January–May 4: Performs at Comedy Theatre, New York, for twenty-week season.
	June: de Bosis begins anti-Fascist activities.
	July–August: Visits de Bosis family in Ancona.
	November 30: de Bosis's mother arrested in Rome.
1931	de Bosis, exiled in Paris, prepares for flight over Rome.
	April 14: Arrives in Paris and learns of de Bosis's plan.
	July–September: In hiding with de Bosis.
	October 3: de Bosis disappears after flight over Rome.
1932	March 13: Death of nephew, Edward C. Carter Jr.
1933	March: Visits Morocco with Aileen Tone, reciting as dinner guest of the Pasha in Marrakesh.
	December: Tours South Africa and Rhodesia through February 19, 1934.
1934	March: Travels through Egypt and Holy Land.

1935	March: Performs in Havana, Cuba.
	Travels through Mexico.
1936	April: Tours Scandinavia.
1938	January–August: Tours India, Ceylon, Burma, Thailand, Malaya, Java, Bali, Australia, New Zealand, and Fiji.
1939	June–August: Visits England and France, with occasional performances.
1940	May–July: Tours South America.
1941–1945	Wartime tours for troops in United States and Canada.
1943	March 24: Death of nephew, Sanders Draper, in RAF.
	June 19: Death of half-sister, Martha L. Draper.
1946	March–July: Returns to England.
	Spends season in London and tours English and Scottish cities for sixteen weeks.
	April 1: Death of Edward Sheldon.
	Recites at Marlborough House before Queen Mary.
	September–October: Returns to Italy and to Paris.
1947	February 8: Death of brother, Charles Dana Draper.
	February 28: Death of Henry James III, son of William James.
1951	June 11: Performs at Windsor Castle.
	July 6: Receives honorary doctor of law degree from University of Edinburgh.
	November 23: Receives honorary CBE from King George VI.
1954	June: Receives honorary doctor of law degree from Cambridge University.
1956	April–July: Travels. Performs in Rome, Holland, Vienna, and London.
	Autumn: Tours United States.
	December 25: Opens two–week season in New York.
	December 30: Dies in sleep.

Other Honorary Degrees:

1924 Hamilton College, New York, honorary master of arts.

1941 University of Maine, Orono, Maine, honorary doctor of fine arts.

1947 Smith College, Massachusetts, honorary doctor of humanities.

THE WORLD OF RUTH DRAPER

Introduction

THE HOUSE LIGHTS DIM, THE AUDIENCE sits quietly, expectantly. Those who have seen Ruth Draper before smile to themselves in anticipation of meeting old friends and, perhaps, a few new ones. Those who have never seen Ruth Draper also wait expectantly—skeptical, eager—well, we'll see. The curtain rises on a bare stage: Deep brown velvet curtains line the three walls; there is a folding chair set stage left. The stage lights are up.

The Lady of the Manor enters, tall, smiling, bowing in welcome. She wears a long, dark brown dress, black lace scarf across her shoulders, a feather boa to be fussed with, enormous, unbelievable hat, strings of pearls and beads, long cream-colored gloves, lace parasol, a beaded reticule hanging from her wrist; and she carries a tortoiseshell lorgnette through which she peers, and with which she gestures and points. She is everyone's favorite aunt, and we all smile in return. The Bazaar is in full swing on the terrace.

After the Parson's speech and prayer and Mr. Floyd's introduction, which is most embarrassing, her Ladyship rises to make her usual speech of welcome, almost forgets to read telegrams from the Duchess, who has an attack of the gout, from the dear Dean, and from her son Cyril, who is with his regiment in India and remembering his old friends; they all wish great success to the Bazaar, which is now declared "Open!"

A small boy named Charlie presents her Ladyship with a bouquet of flowers picked from his mother's garden, which, when he has run off, she finds heavy—and she can't bear carrying a bouquet anyway—and places it on a chair, saying, "Don't let me forget it."

Her voice is warm, cordial, and she is delighted to see her friends from the village. She greets old Mr. Dew in his new wheelchair, admiring the red wheels, "They're so cheerful!" greets the boy scouts in their smart new uniforms, and, nodding right and left, greets a number of others, patronizes the stalls—pot holders, gilded bull-rushes, cream buns—"I'll take the lot!" Then there is Buckle, the old family coachman, who taught her, and all her descendants, to ride and is now their cherished friend. Finally she exits to get her tea before the tea-tent becomes crowded. Often, someone in the audience calls out, concerned, anxious, "Don't forget the bouquet!"

We see them all, feel the warm summer air, and are wrapped in kindness, generosity, the mellow generations of an established event. But she is gone, the Lady of the Manor; all the villagers are gone—the stage is bare. There was no bouquet, although we saw it all; only the brown hangings of the backdrop remain. Miss Draper returns wearing her basic brown stage dress—no glorious hat—and formally, rather stiffly, takes her bows while the audience, suddenly friendly, nod to each other, smiling and comfortable—this is such a secure world, the platitudes so familiar.

In two or three minutes, the curtain rises again. A young English girl wearing a plain smock and broad brimmed Panama hat turned up in front works at her painting in a church in Italy. She and a friend are copying the famous painting of the Madonna della Misericordia. She is all enthusiasm, wide angular gestures, and speaks with her friend in a young, ingenuous English voice about their difficulties, about the colors—"I just love squeezin' paint." Finally, they pack up their painting gear to exit before the old beggar woman works her way to them and all those tourists coming up the aisle. Immediately, a bent old crone, black shawl over her head and shoulders, shuffles along, approaching each group of tourists, and, in a hollow, rasping whine, points out the Madonna and asks, "Un soldino, prego, multo povera, cinque bambini a casa—per l'amor di Dio, prego." Two or three give—"*Tante grazie.*" The next one refuses, and she shuffles off, muttering angrily, with black looks.

In seconds, as we gaze at the arches and gray distances of the church, a group of American tourists appears. The leader, in a long gray linen traveling coat and a plain flat hat, carries an umbrella crooked over her arm and a Baedeker guidebook in its red cover. She reads the measurements and the architectural details in a flat midwestern voice. One senses that her tired group does not really care; they relate everything to their hometown and reminisce about people and incidents of which they are reminded; they discuss their shopping and finally all move off.

They have no sooner gone than from an arch across the aisle, a beautiful young Italian girl, small white lace shawl over her head and carrying a red rose, runs lightly on her toes, searching eagerly for her young man. She finds him, and in a lovely liquid voice breathlessly arranges a meeting on the next day, when she will be able to escape her mother's eye. She crosses herself before the altar, and in a final gesture, raises the rose to her lips, blowing him a kiss. She is gone.

Now enters, in direct fashion, a German tourist—green loden cape, Bavarian felt hat, metal framed glasses, cane, bundles in string bags, large purse. Slowly, she walks down the aisle, confronts the Madonna, and points it out to her party—Gretl, Frieda, and Willy: "Schokolade? Heir, in der Kirche? Nein, Willy!" Impressed and nodding, she gazes respectfully at the painting: "Der kaiser was heir? Ach so. Und Goethe auch?" That they stand where the great men stood reduces her to satisfied silence. Expressing disgust with Italian food—"Macaroni—macaroni—macaroni!"—they go off in search of Münchener Bier.

Slowly, silently, burdened with anxiety, an Italian woman in a large black shawl crosses herself as she passes the altar and again as she sinks to her knees before the Madonna della Misericordia. Eyes closed, with hands clenched in prayer, anguished, she remains for moments while the audience, respectful, silent, almost not breathing, shares her prayer. Gradually, a look of peace comes to her face; her hands relax and open. Slowly the curtain descends, the stage lights dimming.

The audience sits silently, deeply moved, for several moments before the curtain rises and Miss Draper takes her bows, smiling shyly to a storm of applause. Again there had been only Ruth Draper—no church, no groups of tourists, no painting, no easel, no box of paints and brushes.

Both of these character sketches were first presented in the 1920s and remained staples of her repertoire, growing in depth and in economy. *The Bazaar* ran for twenty-five minutes, and in it Ruth Draper played one character who interacted with twenty-seven other characters and various groups, all of whom she evoked. *The Church* ran for thirty minutes. Ruth Draper became six different characters and evoked twenty. Each person in the audience saw the two scenes and recognized all the characters present in the Italian church.

The intense concentration required to project the setting, to convincingly "become" each of the seven characters and to make visible the forty-seven evoked characters, is formidable. When Ruth Draper changed from one character to another, it was as though an electric switch had been lightly tapped. In the blink of an eye, instantly, one character and personality vanished and a different one, equally rounded and tangible, stood in its place.

With more or less brilliance, her character sketches were incisive short stories, Chekhovian in their economy and perception. Perfectly paced, her people came onstage, bearing with them the years of their lives just passed, and proceeded offstage to a continuation of their lives. What the audience saw, for just that period of time, was a fully rounded segment of a whole life.

Perhaps Ruth Draper's greatest genius lay in her ability to so stimulate the audience that it did much of the work through its collective imagination. "I bring the audience up onto the stage with me," she said, and they left the theatre having seen a diversity of characters through her compassionate understanding, for she regarded all people with tolerance, uncritically. "Everybody is rather ridiculous, rather pitiful." Her own character was evident—there was no malice, no evil, no bitterness, no holding up to ridicule—she did not make fun of her people— they were, in themselves, amusing, and the audience recognized itself, its aunts, and its cousins. This sense of recognition is one of the great experiences on either side of the footlights. "It is the duty of the actor," said Sybil Thorndike, "to see to it that the audience which leaves the theatre is not the same audience which entered the theatre." No one left Ruth Draper's theatre untouched; the eye of the beholder held a new vision.

Ruth Draper's unique quality, the quality that set her apart, was her ability to project an illusion, to evoke upon the stage other characters with whom she conversed and interacted. Pure theatre, dramatic power, and imagination come from within. Lynn Fontanne said of this faculty of Ruth's: "There is the flavor of parlor magic in it—something of conjuring." Bernard Levin, drama critic, writing in *The Times* of London on April 4, 1988, recalls Ruth Draper's ability of evocation as "truly hallucinating": "Before the curtain came down, real hallucination had set in and we could see on the stage a crowd of people who were not there!" In 1952, Kenneth Tynan wrote that "this is the most modern group acting" he had ever seen. The old stage doorman, at Ruth's theatre in London, who had seen all the great ones, said: "It is mass hypnotism night after night." And Leo Lerman, in a 1947 *Playbill* in New York, wrote: "After Duse, Ruth Draper is the greatest stage magician of our time." To her audiences, these were real people, "the joint product," Ruth said, "of my own and the audience's imagination."

To understand Ruth Draper in performance, one must accept the fact that she was an inexplicable phenomenon, her talent innate, as much a part of her as her heart or lungs, as automatic as breathing, equally a process of nature.

There is no one against whom Ruth Draper can be judged or compared, for she was like no other. Existing in an inner world of her own, her genius of so personal a quality that it defies definition; she was an original and stood alone, separate and distinct.

The one essential, indispensable element in a Ruth Draper performance was, of course, Ruth Draper herself, for she embodied the inexplicable quality that was her magic. It was this quality of magic, in addition to the quality of the woman herself—of compassion, of humor, of kindness and sympathy toward her characters—that gave Ruth Draper her unique place in the one-woman theatre of her time. This was the quality that set her apart, beyond the usual run of platform entertainers.

How can one dissect such a talent, innate, God given, "the touch," she said, "of a fairy's wand at birth"? Ruth herself could not do so, for it was an unconscious, unpremeditated talent and her natural way of expressing what she wished to communicate. It was not interpretive, as in performing the work of another, but creative. Using her self as an instrument, she "wrote" upon her audiences rather than using a pen upon a sheet of paper. Significantly, without an audience, Ruth found it impossible to perform, which is why not one of her sketches was fully written down. Had it been otherwise, she would have been a Chekhov, a Balzac.

The repertoire of 36 dramatic sketches, from which Ruth Draper drew in her last two or three decades, required that she hold in her mind, in her emotional and physical memory, the detailed image of 52 characters that she performed, as well as the 316 that she evoked. These 36 sketches, in the playing time of their complete texts, totaled about nine hours and twenty minutes—the equivalent of four full-length plays. She could summon any one character at a moment's notice and perform without reflection, transforming herself instantly into the person she had built in her mind; this could be done under any condition and the most unlikely of circumstances. To be asked to get up before a small group in a friend's drawing room or before a party on a picnic was no more than if someone said, "Ruth, tell us a story." It was all simple, natural, and unselfconscious. Her sister Alice said, "Ruth held her talents as a sacred trust, not as a means of gaining acclaim for herself."

Introduction

The monologue is a special form of acting, a dramatic composition for a single performer evoking other characters upon the stage. Over the years of theatre history, from Ancient Greece to television, there have been many practitioners—the list is long, and the variations are many. Most would be considered "platform entertainers," and the usual vehicle was farce or comedy, mimicry—imitation and impersonation—or the dramatic reading.

In the late 1970s, the solo performer turned in a different direction, turned, largely, to the world of biography: Hal Holbrook as Mark Twain, Pat Carroll as Gertrude Stein, Emlyn Williams as Dylan Thomas or as Charles Dickens, Zoe Caldwell as Lillian Hellman. All were remarkable impersonations, some were uncannily "like," and all carried substance and power. Now, in the 1990s, solo performers like Lily Tomlin, Whoopi Goldberg, Tracey Ullman, and Eric Bogosian have developed comedy monologues to create their own collection of character sketches. Only Bogosian writes his own script.

Solo performers usually had been trained actors with solid experience in stage plays. Ruth Draper, on the contrary, was untrained and without stage experience of any kind. When she did attempt to act with others, she found it limiting, uncongenial, rather disturbing, and notably unsuccessful. Ruth Draper, however, had one unique quality: her unshakable conviction that she embodied, had actually become, the character she imagined and that the words and gestures, therefore, came directly from the character portrayed. Not written down, the entire concept was in her mind—and so remained fluid, never losing the spontaneity of reality.

They did not come instantly, her people, full blown. An idea would occur to her, and it would be months, often years, before it became fully shaped in her imagination, shaped, she said, without conscious direction. As the character developed in her mind, so the situation grew, written from the inside out. She claimed not to rehearse privately, before a mirror, but would "try it out" on family, on friends. "I've got a new idea," she would say. "Tell me what you think of it." And as she became the character in action, gestures, bits of business, remarks came spontaneously, and the new persona lived. The imagined character could not be performed until she herself had taken it over.

Judge Learned Hand, who knew Ruth well, said: "She seemed to have lived countless lives and remembered them all; she had to have the whole creation of her people as though she must transmute her own being into anothers." She sought only accuracy, from which came comedy, sometimes tragedy, but always truth. In the belief of her audience, truth was confirmed; and if "Truth," onstage, is the result of effect, so be it—taken all together it was the perfected illusion that spelled "Truth."

"I have to live with a sketch for two, three or five years before I am sure it has something to it." Words, accents, phrases, gestures, all were carefully calculated—however spontaneous—tested before her family and friends, selected, simplified, revised, reworked. Finally performed, her characterizations were held loosely, alive, growing in richness of detail as over the years they met a variety of audiences, developing the familiar, the casual, the average, becoming recognizable. A sketch performed in the 1950s would be quite different from its original version of thirty or forty years earlier. The basic story line and characterization remained constant, but the dialogue with the people she evoked was fluid and influenced by the response of her audience. "If the audience is exciting and lively, intelligent and responsive" then she would respond to them spontaneously in lively fresh words and phrasing, a new gesture or piece of business. "Sometimes I am startled by a good line—but I can never remember it!" Often lines were not lost and went into the script of her memory. She worked at her characters with each performance, simplifying her portraits, strengthening, always refining to make the image sharper.

Ruth Draper was conscious, as is any performer, of the mood and reactions of the audience. Each one had a personality, and she loved her audiences as she loved her friends. Scottish audiences "are *amazing*, such a grand, generous, *adorable* public and so sparkling and intelligent—it's pure joy to play to them . . . just thrilling!" The audience in Manchester, England, two thousand every show, "perhaps the best public in the world, they are *so* quick, so vital, sincere and intelligent, responding with a speed and warmth that carries one beyond one's own capacity. I never had more fun!" And of London, Oxford, and Cambridge, she wrote: "Marvellous audiences and I gave a good show in consequence."

To a fine point, Ruth Draper knew how well she performed. Coming offstage one night, she whipped by her stage manager saying, "My! I was *good*—wasn't I?" To a friend who wrote another time of her enjoyment, Ruth replied, "I did not 'feel' I was very good that day. I was not much inspired by the audience—had I known you were in it I should have done better, I know."

Ruth Draper's characterizations were not learned by rote, word perfect; "they were kept alive," said Alexander Woollcott, in the *The New Yorker*, "by constant alteration, so that some of the older ones became as mellow and rich as an old Meershaum pipe. They were perfected dramatic portraits." It was this quality of freshness, of spontaneous conversation with the people she evoked, that made her performances always a new revelation. Her audience came time and again to enjoy their old friends, who never grew static or stale. "She understands," said Wolcott Gibbs, also in *The New Yorker*, "the peculiar aborting of syntax, the carefree imprecision in the use of words, the inconsequence of thought. Her humor is a matter of extreme subtlety and ingenuity . . . tragedy and comedy exist simultaneously in time and space . . . the command of language and vernacular is impressive."

Mahlon Niall wrote to Alice: "Ruth Draper's ability to shed light on so many aspects of human behavior and over such an enormous range is what gives her work such remarkable stature and power. To create insight, or to distract an audience is the difference between and artist and an entertainer. Ruth Draper could do both, but even her entertaining, brilliant as it was, was never mere distraction. That is what kept us coming back, year after year! . . . She is so warm, so truly alive, and she projects this so marvelously."

The monologue is one of the most exacting forms of entertainment. In speaking of her own work, Ruth Draper said: "For the young actress I don't think it is a form of acting which should be encouraged because it can't be anything but slightly embarrassing if a person does it with too much effort. It has to be a natural gift. A great many people try to do what I do but are always looking for material that others write for them. I believe in my form of acting doing one's own creations is very important. I've never been able to do anything I myself haven't written." And then, there is one essential quality: "I have had very good health and great vitality which I think is the most important gift that any artist can have."

Onstage, Ruth Draper was a presence—vital, strong, sure, and commanding the whole theatre, whether the Coliseum in London, a Variety Hall in Manchester or Liverpool, or a smaller, more intimate theatre. In performance she was totally relaxed, not in any way conscious of herself, her concentration completely upon the character she had become. At curtain time, taking her bow, she was brisk and businesslike, dignified and appreciative, often shyly moved.

"I believe," she wrote in 1927, "that all experience and all pain is but grist to my mill, to be used in laughter or beauty or whatever it may be, for the delight of others and the deepening of my own nature and accomplishment."

Walter Starkie wrote Ruth Draper in 1932, saying: "You are one of the only people except Duse who can produce drama by your immobility as well as by your movement."

After performing for Duse in her hotel suite in Milan in 1922, Ruth asked her: "When you make yourself so tall on stage, how do you do it?" And Duse replied that she had asked Bernhardt the same question and Bernhardt said, "Ask Ruth Draper."

"You *are* theatre," said Duse to Ruth.

Ruth Draper never left the social world of the Draper family nor the cosmopolitan—mostly English—social world that appreciated, marveled, and welcomed her. She simply "stepped out to the theatre to work." She did not become part of the theatre world, although the theatre greats came to marvel, too, at her performances. Somehow she made a fusion of her several worlds, perhaps because she remained incorruptibly herself.

Ruth Draper was not a large woman, but she was a force. As a child, she had been small, thin, lacking vigor, and completely overshadowed by a large and vigorous family. She grew to five feet four inches, compact and strong, her forces centered within herself, reserved, controlled. She grew to be handsome and elegant, with a fine sense of her own style, and could be strikingly beautiful, her large brown eyes sparkling and instantly expressive. Though she did not suffer fools at all, she had a real talent for friendship; her greatest happiness lay in giving pleasure to others. With an appealing shy charm, she yet was a formidable personality not to be trifled with.

In her personal life, too, Ruth was an original. With supreme self-confidence, she established for herself, long before it was the accepted, usual thing, her woman's independence. No less than Edith Wharton, of similar background, she was a pioneer. She lived her own life, made her own way, arrived at her own decisions, and maintained her unshakable integrity in every aspect of her life. Aside from her great talent, she was unique, a fascinating, complex woman who, in her forties, had a brief but intense and dramatic love affair with a much younger man who became an anti-Fascist martyr.

These pages attempt to illuminate the woman who was Ruth Draper and the world she built for herself

1

Beginnings

TWO DAYS PAST HER SEVENTY-SECOND birthday, on December 4, 1956, a party was given for Ruth Draper in Chicago, where she was on tour. Cornelia Conger describes it:

> John and Nina Wilson gave the party. It was all that Ruth loved—about 120 people of her own world—in the right setting—she the guest of honor receiving with them. She sat at dinner with three of our most distinguished and attractive men around her, one on each side and one just across the narrow table—many warm old friends to greet her. "It is so long since I have given my monologues at a party like this," she said, and seemed happy and excited. She wore her lovely brocade dress and her hair had just been waved in an especially becoming line. She wore her little rose-red slippers and carried the matching velvet wrap that she wore in the "Actress" monologue—she looked *very* beautiful and I never saw her so radiant and her wonderful eyes were shining—I think she gave the most brilliant performance I can recall. She seemed on fire and held her audience breathless. It was a group who seemed to miss none of her gentle satire, none of her glancing asides. I—who have seen her so often—amused myself now and then by watching their faces—I never saw such complete absorption, such quick response, nor more whole-hearted appreciation!
>
> As she had to catch an 11:15 train, Nina Wilson had planned the whole party with greatest care so she would not be hurried or anxious, and had brought her own maid to the Club to help Ruth change and pack. Nina's car was waiting to drive her to the train and one of her friends, Jack Murphy, drove down with her to put her aboard. Ruth chose *The Scottish Immigrant* as her final piece as she did not want to be delayed by people swarming around her at the end. There was a center aisle and the little stage was only a step up—so as she sighted "her Sandy" she jumped down, ran down the aisle waving and

calling "Sandy, my Sandy," and was out of the room and in the dressing room before anyone realized it!"

Twenty years earlier, Ruth had written, "Courage, enthusiasm, awareness, if only one can keep these to the end." Keep them she did, throughout her incredibly active life, kept them triumphantly, beyond doubt, almost beyond endurance. Her awareness and enthusiasm never faltered; she had the courage to go on, but not the courage to stop.

Three weeks later, Ruth Draper opened in New York, on Broadway, on Christmas night. She was "very tired and a little bit scared." Between Tuesday night and Saturday night, she played seven performances, exiting as the same *Scottish Immigrant*, the character for which she had the greatest feeling, her first real creation. She seemed as young in her playing in 1956 as she had forty years before.

After many curtain calls, Ruth Draper was driven home in her car, the standing, shouting ovation ringing in her ears, driven past the Christmas lights in Rockefeller Center to her apartment on East 79th Street, to her post-performance supper, and went to bed. About seven o'clock the next morning, she died quietly in her sleep. Until the end, she had kept those qualities she cherished, to the last night she was onstage.

Ruth was not yet eight as she sat cross-legged on a window seat in the top-floor schoolroom of the big forty-foot brownstone house at 19 East 47th Street in New York. She was quite oblivious to the games of her five brothers and sisters because she was in another self—in the self of the Jewish tailor who came several times a year to alter or to make new clothes for the children. "A pathetic, lovely little man," Ruth recalled him many years later. As she sat there, a shawl across her thin little shoulders, bent over her imaginary sewing, she sniffled and coughed and talked to herself of tucks and pleats, of letting out and taking in, of shorter this and longer that; pure mimicry, but it was observed and true, and she was wholly absorbed in her pretending.

Strongly individual, Ruth was observant, quiet, busy in her own mind. The others recognized and accepted her difference and her pretending, which entertained them all as she became the tailor, the seamstress, Fraulein, or renewed memories of a channel crossing; they begged for their favorites and shrieked with delight. Soon she had to come downstairs to entertain her mother's visitors: "*Really*, that *child*" But Ruth would remain apart, always different from the others, and with an inner loneliness and reserve that few penetrated, although she would be surrounded always by warm and close relationships.

On both sides of her family, Ruth was of English stock, her first ancestors arriving in America before 1650. She inherited eight generations of New England virtue and the Puritan qualities that were so strong a part of her character: self-reliant independence, hard work, thrift, strong ethical and moral standards, strength of purpose. "If only I knew God's will I would gladly obey," she would say in moments of unsettling ambivalence as to the direction of her life, often remarking, "the locality of our origin has much to account for." It was all in her genes, for she had no actual foothold in her grandfathers' New England soil.

Ruth's father and her mother's father (only eleven years apart in age) came from large families in New Hampshire and Vermont, worked their way through college, and were each outstanding in his profession, widely read, interested in the arts, concerned with people. Her grandfather, Charles Anderson Dana, educated at Harvard College, healthy, vigorous, intelligent, broadly experienced in public affairs, in the early 1860s managing editor at *The New York Tribune* under Horace Greeley, became part owner and editor of *The New York Sun* in 1868. Over the next thirty years, he became known as a brilliant liberal journalist, his years as assistant secretary of war in Lincoln's cabinet giving him insight into government. In 1846 he had married Eunice McDaniel of an old Maryland family. Achieving wealth and position, he built a large mansion at 60th Street on the northwest corner of Madison Avenue, where he collected paintings and Chinese porcelains— one of the first such collections in New York. At Dosoris Island, near Glen Cove on Long Island, he developed fine gardens and horticultural studies.

Ruth Dana, the second daughter of Eunice and Charles Dana, married William Henry Draper in December 1877. He was twenty years older than she and eight years a widower, with a son and daughter then aged fourteen and thirteen. In the next nine years, Ruth Dana Draper gave him six more children, three sons and three daughters. Because of a bad heart, she had been educated at home and by travel abroad. Probably very like her father, she was intelligent, strong-minded, dominant in character, and with broad interests. Accustomed in her father's house to men of accomplishment and distinction, and to talk of the world's affairs, she brought a dimension to the life of her own children that their home might otherwise have lacked.

William Henry Draper, however, could hold his own. Handsome and of standing and influence in his profession, he undoubtedly was master in his own house. He had taken his medical degree in 1855 at the College of Physicians and Surgeons and as a professor of clinical medicine there became an outstanding teacher with an adventurous and searching mind. He was a general practitioner of unusual diagnostic skill.

William Henry Draper had married, first, Elizabeth Kinnicutt of Worcester, Massachusetts, but she died at twenty-nine. Their two children were William Kinnicutt Draper, born in 1863, and his sister, Martha Lincoln Draper, a year younger. Then, in 1879, began the second family with Charles, George, Dorothea, and Alice, all slightly more than a year apart, Ruth, born December 2, 1884, and Paul, two years younger. Thus there was an age spread of twenty-three years with a variety of activities and interests all going on at the same time in the same household.

Dosoris, the Dana home at Glen Cove, in summer and the house at 25 East 60th Street in winter were, so long as the grandparents lived, the hub of the families, with the grandchildren continually in and out. Several times a week, Charles

Dana, walking downtown on his way to his office at *The Sun*, would stop at 47th Street to look in on the Drapers gathered at the breakfast table. There was constant communication.

In about 1881/1882, Ruth Dana Draper wrote to Charles Dana:

> Dear Pa, I think that I admire my children more when I think about you, for it may be that they will carry on the sort of life and the thoughts and the face that have been always in you. It is a beautiful fact how entirely my mind and hopes seem to work with my children. It must be so with everybody, but it seems to be an entirely natural instinct to put your chief strength and aim into them so that at once comes the greatest satisfaction in life. I hope that it will not all smash up. Charles is not quite so bad as he has been and I have some hope of him. They are the most beautiful things that ever were seen, and they are getting on well in strength and growth. There is one thing that seriously troubles me. So far as my own development is concerned, as I look back I seem to refer to you in all that I have learned, and for the strengthening of right in me, and for the capacity of enjoying most things that stick by me now, and for the general use that I have of my mind. I know that if my children were near you they would find the same impetus in you that ever gave me a push to be not a fool. It seems to me that even more you would help them along, because you have become interested more in Nature, so that my young children could love what you are doing better than they could cyclopedias or poetry books. . . . I wish you would think about it, for they are such very nice children that you would really like to see them yourself. . . . We are going to have your grand-daughter christened this afternoon. I am not yet sure of her name, but will let my family know as soon as possible. She is a very handsome person.

Highly individualistic, the Draper children were a volatile, vibrant mix, but Ruth and her brother Paul—two years younger—seem to have been in a separate category. Imaginative, the artists of the family, inseparable companions, always role-playing, often joined by their exact contemporary, Malvina Hoffman, also an artist and the daughter of Joseph Hoffman, a well-known pianist. Ruth and Paul, the babies of the family, in summer often sitting at their own table in the dining room during family dinners, neither really grew up—Ruth, particularly, retained always the innocence and purity of a child, and Paul his irresponsibility. Dr. and Mrs. Draper were always present at the family lunch table—which must have formed its own collegial training ground. Sunday morning they all lined up for Dr. Draper to be sure that each had a fresh pocket handkerchief and money for the plate. They must have made a tight fit in their Grace Church pew.

There was music and laughter and great fun—but strict discipline. Music was a daily force. Paul and Dorothea had good voices and became active in the musical world. Ruth, though neither singing nor playing, became a passionate, en-thralled listener and devoted friend of many musicians, furthering their careers in many small ways. George performed on the musical saw.

Siblings, cousins, and friends abounded. "Mrs. Draper was kind to all visiting children," one child remembered many years later. "There was a gay sweep to the way she did things." The nurse of the four neighboring Boit sisters, in reprimand-ing them, used to say, "Little Ruth Draper wouldn't do that." And they cordially hated little Ruth Draper. But when little Alice Boit visited the Drapers for a few days, she found that "little Ruth Draper did *all* that." Alice Boit knew Ruth in their childhood as shy, with great brown eyes, living "in a world of her own be-lieving; even as a small child she played a role." This role playing continued as a game, a defense, a protection or armor for her insecurity and became the basis of her stage career.

As a child, Ruth did not have the vigor and stamina she later developed; she appeared frail, "almost rickety," one of her sisters said. And Mrs. Draper regularly sent to a Harlem farm for goat's milk to strengthen her. Gertrude Homer, a sum-mer neighbor in Maine, wrote many years later, "I so well remember Ruth then as a rather pathetic, thin unattractive girl who was completely overshadowed by a very attractive family." The Drapers were an unusually strong and cohesive unit within the Draper and Dana families. In Ruth's generation there were thirty-one first cousins, the then eldest of them writing in 1943: "Such a happy lot of cous-ins we have been! It has been a nearly perfect lifelong relationship of affection and companionship such as few families are lucky enough to have. I can't see anywhere that anything like what we all had together is coming to the younger generation. We have been lucky." All these relationships were active, close, and nourishing and provided a rich soil in which to grow up.

The girls were educated at home by governesses and by their mother—three to four hours of lessons each day. Later, Dorothea attended Miss Spence's School at 6 West 48th Street, where Ruth followed her for one year (1895–96) and for six weeks the next fall.

Temperamentally, Ruth was not suited to the ordered lessons and school en-vironment. Nothing caught her imagination, and she reacted, Dorothea said, by being "very naughty indeed." At this point Mrs. Draper found Hannah Henrietta Hefter, "a funny little old German woman" who understood the twelve-year-old child and lit the spark: languages, literature, history, books and pictures and muse-ums. This began Ruth's real education, and to the end of her life she eagerly looked and inquired and listened. She would never lose the excitement of learning.

This was acceptable teaching for girls in 1896, and when in 1924 Hamilton College would award Ruth an honorary degree of master of arts, the citation noted that she was "educated not by any college, but by [her] inheritance of all the best that the culture of our greatest city affords." Ruth's education depended, signifi-cantly, upon cultural awareness rather than upon the amassing of facts. The long travels of her professional career, in addition to the richness of the friendships she formed, would provide a breadth of association with people in music, in literature, and in the arts, which she would eagerly grasp.

Ruth, however, would be quite aware of the inadequacies of her upbringing. In 1956, from Sorrento, she would write to Dorothea: "I make everybody laugh at my Italian, which in a way sounds like the real thing, and is confusing, being full of mistakes and wrong words. How I regret never having been *made* to *work* at anything! Darling Barie tried hard to make me apply myself to lessons, when she helped me as a child, but never succeeded!"

The Draper children grew up as New Yorkers, in the next generation of the established social world described by Edith Wharton and Henry James. They grew up with the younger generation of the inner circle: Iselin, Griswold, Schuyler, Roosevelt and Kean, Tuckerman, Fish, Auchincloss, King and Jay. New York was smaller in those days, closer, more wary of newcomers, but Charles Dana and Dr. Draper had attained a solid position in the life of the city, and all doors were open to their children.

In Boston, they were equally favored with Henry Adams, his Hooper nieces and William James, the Endicott Peabodys, the Howes and Higginsons as family friends, and other Bostonians who also came to the Maine coast in the summer.

Music had brought Dr. and Mrs. Draper together, and music was an ever-present element in their home. In later years, George remembered roller skating home from school one warm day with his brother Charles, and as they came down the block they could see the curtains blowing out of the open windows and hear their mother playing two-part piano sonatas with Paderewski. He had come to New York in 1891, on his first American tour, and was staying at the Hotel Windsor on the corner of Fifth Avenue and 47th Street. Dr. Draper had been recommended for the removal of a felon on his finger. Hearing Mrs. Draper playing upstairs, Paderewski asked to be presented and rapidly became a family friend; Mrs. Draper did much to further his concert career in New York. In her large forty-foot drawing room, with its two concert-grand pianos, she gave many musical parties and small concerts. For a number of years, she held weekly musical evenings at which young musicians were heard and received her criticism and encouragement.

The first crack in the solid bulwark of the family came with the death, at seventy-one, of Dr. Draper on April 26, 1901. Grace Church, on the morning of May 6, was crowded for his funeral service. *The Columbia Spectator* said: "He was a family doctor and his force of character, breadth of charm and personality, made him an exceptionally fine teacher." Sir William Osler, a Canadian physician renowned both in England and the United States, wrote of Dr. Draper in *The New York Times* on April 27, 1901: "One felt a trustfulness in his honesty and a faith in his convictions. A voice of uncommon sweetness, a singularly attractive face and a winning manner lent special charms to him as a speaker. . . . In all respects the ideal physician [he had] rare grace of presence and a quiet dignity and reserve. A genial and unfailing courtesy and sweetness of manner gave him an unrivaled popularity. He was beloved by his patients and esteemed by his pupils and colleagues."

Many years later Ruth was to say, "I was born and grew up in the lap of the medical profession and I feel in a very definite way that my education and preparation for life were closely connected with it and deeply influenced by it." She thought of her father's distinguished associates, men of accomplishment and renown, whom she looked on "with awe and admiration, many with deep affection. One does not forget such men; they set a standard for all one's life."

Mrs. Draper was left a vigorous widow of fifty-one. Formidably established as the daughter of Charles A. Dana and the widow of the well-loved Dr. Draper, she kept a firm grip on her social life, maintaining her position and prestige in New York. "Ma went to Aunt Ella's for dinner and sat between J.P.M. [J. P. Morgan] and Mr. Lanier, and after dinner the Mayor [Seth Low] chose her for a long talk." From Washington, where she was staying with Mrs. Elihu Root, Mrs. Draper wrote, "I propose to return on Friday, having been asked to the President [Theodore Roosevelt] at luncheon on Thursday." The consciousness in the next generation of "who we are" surely stemmed from Ruth Dana Draper's attitude and self-esteem.

With the death of her husband, Mrs. Draper was unquestionably the dominant, unchallenged head of the family, her "pride of place" given full rein. Her sons Charles and George were at Harvard, Paul a fifteen-year-old schoolboy at Groton, and the girls still at home. Mrs. Draper sold the East 47th Street house, where they had lived since 1883 and where Ruth and Paul had been born, and bought a double house at 18 West 8th Street, just a few blocks from her friends the Duncans at No. 1 Fifth Avenue. Paul Dana, her brother, had married a Duncan daughter.

"Bossy" with the children, a stern disciplinarian, and very critical, she could be sharply sarcastic for, with her red hair, she had a quick temper and "a tongue that cut like a knife." George never forgot watching his brother Charles's frantic attempt to climb up an armoire, out of reach of his mother, who came after him with a switch and "beat the daylights out of him" for some misbehavior. One senses from family letters that Charles, as soon as he was old enough, kept his own life out of his mother's ken. Ruth, too, received a rebuke in the form of a letter (still existing) written on scraps of torn up letters, bills, and other remnants from the wastebasket, pinned together, to point out her lapse in ordering notepaper at a time when she was learning to run the house.

Alice Boit Burnham, who grew up with the Drapers, told this writer that Mrs. Draper and her children were sharply, outspokenly critical—of each other and of everyone else. This seems not to have cast much of a shadow on their mutual loving relationships so deeply concerned with each other's welfare—warm, but wary. They all had humor, of sorts, ranging variously from Ruth's sense of the ridiculous to the real wit of Mrs. Draper and Dorothea—sharp and ruthless. This must have toughened them all but been more than a little disconcerting to those on the periphery of the family core group. A special Draper-family language surely added to the discomfort.

At this time (1902–3), Ruth's eighteenth birthday was fast approaching. She

did not look with pleasure upon the formalities of being "presented to society"—
her mother's friends and social acquaintances—and the year or more of debutante
parties for all their daughters: teas, dinners, dances, and balls. She seized upon the
idea of boarding school, of being forced to work: "For the past few years I certainly have not been severely treated." She wanted a year to study, but then she
would be just twenty in 1904–5. "Is that too old?" she asked Dorothea. "Perhaps
not for me. I do want a year to myself. You understand, though you may not sym-
pathize!" In the event, she remained at home. She found it difficult; what she really
wanted was to pace her activities to her younger brother, Paul, and his friends. "It
would be nice if I were his younger sister and it would be easier for him too. But
I'm so silly and always wishing things were otherwise." She worked for the Junior
League and the various activities of her group, and in the winter of 1903–04, Ruth
"came out," a debutante of just nineteen, as her mother wished.

During these years, her daughters found Mrs. Draper very trying. In February 1903, Ruth wrote to Dorothea, again in Europe:

> Aunt Ella says we're known as the Draper family *and* Mrs. Draper. I
> believe Mrs. Draper says she talked with Miss Georgie Schuyler who
> agrees with her that it's eminently proper for the mother to remain
> in the room. Alice meekly says that perhaps that's the way Miss Georgie
> was brought up and that's the reason she's Miss Georgie! We are not
> mad with Ma, it's such an old story now and Ma says she'll do any-
> thing we want (though she'll forget when the charmers come). . . .
> We've had amusing talks with Ma on the subject of being left alone
> with men who come. George is killing [about it] and it happens that
> I've heard of several people who were talking about the hopelessness
> of seeing the Drapers in anything but bunches! . . . But it's really hope-
> less. The other day Bogart came. Ma had had her tea and left the room
> to say good-bye to someone, which gave her a fine chance. Bogert
> and I were just started on a most delightful talk—I being rather sad
> and so glad to have a caller—when back bounces Ma, sits down and
> for half an hour discourses with him on the value of knowing French
> while I sit absolutely dumb, behind the kettle, embarrassingly quiet
> and out of place and wishing I were upstairs doing Art Notes. My, I
> was discouraged but I didn't scold at all. Later came Harry, but I had
> gone upstairs and they called me down just at the last, to listen to
> them talking about the Panama Canal.

Over the next several years, she wrote repeatedly: "No one of interest has
been here lately. . . . Nobody ever comes to call. Is Ma making herself too charming?" In 1946 Ruth wrote to Alice: "Do you remember tea on 8th Street and how
mother and darling Barie always hung around with the three of us if we had a
gentleman caller?"

In spite of "Ma's charm," however, Alice became engaged. Alice, the quiet sister who cared nothing for society, the only one to go to college, was married, in August 1908 at Dark Harbor, to Edward Clark Carter. They had met some years before at a Christian Movement Conference at Barnard College; Mrs. Draper must have had doubts, for she sent Alice off on a trip around the world with the Bishop of Massachusetts and Mrs. Malcolm Peabody—travel, the classic cure for girls in love. Also of New England background, a graduate of Harvard in 1900, where he played on the Lacrosse team, Edward Carter was five years older than Alice and well established in the international work of the YMCA. He was in India when Alice's tour brought her there, and he sent roses to greet her at every stop; he followed her to Japan, and when he returned to New York early in 1908, Edward was determined to win her. Informed of their wish to marry, Mrs. Draper asked that they not communicate for six months. On the very day, six months later, Alice received a telegram that read, "May I start?" They were married on August 5, and Alice was to find herself moving and settling and moving again for the next fifteen years. With simplicity and intelligence, she worked to do what she could, within the limitations of her influence, for the betterment of conditions as she found them. Above all, she was to do her job as Edward's wife.

As the only one of the children steadily at home during these years, Ruth was smothered by the vigor and force of her mother's determined personality. Ma knew what was best and had all the standards of protectiveness and authority of the Victorian matron. It is small wonder that Ruth often sat quietly in a social group, speaking little, and at a dinner party often made no attempt to keep up her end of the social conversation. In later years, at the height of her career, she developed her social skills and, though no less shy and self-effacing, could be a delight—particularly with those who interested her, whether simple people or ones in the higher echelons of birth or accomplishment; equally she could be outrageously rude.

It also is no wonder that as a child Ruth had been mawkishly sentimental toward her sister Dorothea and appears to have turned to her for understanding. Even at twenty-two, she wrote Dorothea, "I long for a snuggle and a tender word." And again: "I have been very sick of heart lately, but I'm tightening up again now. I wish for you often."

Travel was an important part of Mrs. Draper's life and in her education of her children. From only one of these trips—in 1909—are Ruth's letters extant. She was then twenty-four.

Late in March they sailed for a three-month tour, Mrs. Draper, Ruth, and Mrs. Draper's maid, old Lizzie, "hugely excited and very helpful and good." There were friends on board. Ruth wrote: "I saw my name in 'The Times,' as dancing with Mr. R. I did—we really had a bully time together—he and Ma had long talks and walks and I got very fond of Kermit." No need to put *bully* in quotation marks, the characteristic word of Theodore Roosevelt. Living up to his promise, T. R. had refused to run for what would, in effect, have been a third term as president—in spite of public clamor for him to do so. To promptly remove himself from the political scene, he was now on his way to an African safari with his second son, Kermit, then aged nineteen.

Beginnings

At Naples, George Draper met his mother and Ruth. He brought a cable announcing the sudden marriage of Paul Draper to Muriel Sanders. "Mother is entirely calm and philosophical," Ruth wrote. "We have not let ourselves wonder and think too much until we have more details. I only know those words keep beating in me every minute and I suppose they do with Ma too, but she is not at all broken. . . . It was too good for words to meet George smiling on the dock. He told me at once and I confess I almost sank through the floor of the Dogana; we told Ma a few hours later after a lovely drive and tea and tortoiseshell shopping and a visit to the Aquarium! She was too wonderful and evidently not much shocked. I am sure it had crossed her mind before." And she added, "I can't bare [*sic*] to break off."

At the Hotel Beau Site in Rome, they spent two weeks sightseeing and visiting friends; they took a carriage drive out to the Campagna to see Wright fly his airplane—but that day he did not fly; they took tea with the American sculptor, Moses Ezekiel, in his studio in the Baths of Diocletian. On the very first afternoon they had driven to the Forum, which "affected me to tears tho' I controlled them for I knew George would laugh if he caught me . . . I hope I can wean him a little, for perhaps you know how deeply and chokingly thrilled I am at being here and seeing these things, and it will be difficult if I can't explode at times. We have glorious times giggling tho' I tease him a lot and it's too wonderful seeing him and such a joy to Ma. Gosh, I'm glad he's here."

Probably it was on an earlier trip to the Forum, for the children were younger then and she had more of them with her, that Mrs. Draper left them standing below and climbed slowly up and up and up, stopped, looked carefully about at the stones for a moment, bent down, looked again, and then slowly descended. Years before, she explained, when quite young, she had taken a brick (stone) from the Forum. Now she had returned it to its exact spot. Her conscience would no longer be troubled.

There were many friends visiting Rome, a number of "charmers" from New York, and they all visited the sights and heard "Il Trovatore." "I did monologues between the acts in the back of the tiny box, knees all wedged in close—they would have them." The high Anglican Church service on Easter morning gave her no comfort, and she longed for "a nice, plain American service." Like tourists anywhere and always, they kept "running into friends at the Bank," and there appeared to be a lively group for Ruth and George "to bum around with."

Orvieto, Siena, San Gimignano, and Florence followed, and on to Venice, then Padua, Verona, Milan, the well-worn route. From Florence Ruth wrote to Dorothea to announce, on April 30:

> . . . the acquisition of a string of pearls at Settepassis, on the bridge looking up the Arno to San Miniato bathed in the evening sunlight, Mother and I chose the pearls. They are small, as suits my personality, stature and station, but round and a very pretty color and glow. It cost $476.00! $350.00 from mother, $26.00 from George (from

the salary to come) and the rest in presents of money to me. Of course, I suffered with my conscience. It seemed vain, selfish, useless, beyond my station, too good for me, etc., etc. as if the money should go to something else but on the other hand pearls are a good investment and it pleased mother a lot to give them to me, and I shall always in my sentimental way be glad they came from Florence on this journey of Ma's and George's and mine.

Ruth tried to restrain her mother's somewhat haphazard shopping. "Ma wanted four small bronze horses like the ones on San Marco." In Florence there was a coat from Luzzini, which had to be altered: "It was awful!" In Milan she at once ordered a suit from Ventura's. In Paris "she is now on her way to the 3/4 to try and return an embroidered dress and a huge and awful scarf which she has decided were mistakes!"

This was not the way Ruth shopped. "I find the subject of clothes so ever-present to one's mind," she wrote from Paris. "And the awful question of selections, economies, etc., bewilders me fearfully—and the cost is awful when it comes to 'l'addition!'"

This could have been written by Ruth twenty years—forty years—later. As she became a public figure she shopped carefully, at the best places, resistant unless pleased, reluctant even when pleased, usually somewhat bewildered, and the cost always too great.

In Paris they heard Paderewski at the Conservatoire: "He played his best but seemed very nervous and tired." They saw "Isadora [Duncan] and some wonderful Russian dancers." This was the Paris season in which Diaghilev first presented the Ballet from St. Petersburg, changing artistic perceptions dramatically and forever, but Ruth was too inexperienced to understand its importance.

Then came word of the birth to Alice Carter of twin sons. "It is very hard for mother not to be at home and she will not be contented to stay here now, thinking of the move from the hospital to where? And the need for her service and society to arrange, help with the babies and plan for the rest of the summer."

Mrs. Draper finished her shopping and fittings and crossed to London. Her great friend Jessie Duncan Phipps was out of town, but they saw Mrs. Yates Thompson with whom they went to Cambridge for the Darwin Centenary and the great reception of the Darwin family. Old Lady Ritchie (Anne Thackery) was with them; she "had a big garden hat in a bandbox in the train going down and returning!"

"I really would rather come with Ma; three weeks in London will suit me and I don't want to hang about with Mrs. Thompson and Mrs. Leavitt and Mrs. Rathbone and Mrs. Phipps for a hot month when I might be home having a good time." Mrs. Draper sailed quickly on June 9, and Ruth followed in the "Adriatic" on July 7 as originally planned by her mother.

While still in her late teens, Ruth had sent Dorothea a copy-book exhortation to take every opportunity to travel and to learn; she sent lists of paintings to see, asked for photographs of particular paintings, and begged Dorothea to look at ones she herself had missed on previous trips, or only recently heard about. "Your postal has come!!! My, it's wonderful to think of your having seen all those things. How I'd like to talk it over with you." She was glad that Janet Dana (Dorothea was abroad with Uncle Paul Dana and his family) "is enthusiastic; it makes me so happy that now she will understand! But are you tiring under Uncle Paul's nervous vigor? I fancy he's as exasperating as I am, in a way."

By 1909 Ruth could list every "sight" in every gallery and museum; she knew the names if not always the spelling. "I have no room left for enthusiastic descriptions" she wrote Dorothea, now at home. "I suppose you are delighted."

At every opportunity on these trips, they went to the opera, to the theatre, to concerts, and to museums and galleries, led by their mother who said, "Don't look at that—look at this!" Thus Ruth formed a pattern of constant, repetitious sightseeing and emotional response to beauty and to personal or historical association. With her need to travel, to meet new people, this was to become an essential life force and the basis of her happiness in the tours that were to fill the years of her professional career.

Forty-seven years after this trip, in the last summer of her life, after countless revisiting, she remained deeply stirred by places and views and paintings seen again and again and again until they had become "beloved old friends" whom she needed to see once more. It was an emotional hunger never to be satisfied.

This was the background, these the influences that formed and nurtured the Draper children. From the chrysalis of this happy environment, Ruth slowly emerged to enjoy the last years of the world she had known and that was so soon to end.

2

Emergence

PADEREWSKI HAD SPOKEN WITH RUTH'S parents about her obvious talent, her extraordinary gift of creating an entirely extraneous character within
herself. He spoke of the protection and nurturing of such a talent and of its great
potential. Now, in 1910, when she was twenty-five, he spoke of this directly with
Ruth and urged her to consider a professional career, to develop beyond "parlor
entertainment" for friends and charity. He spoke seriously to her as an artist, about
wider horizons. "Mind you," he said, "I am not advising that you should go to
Paris to study. You may not need training. *You* must make the decision. It must
come from you, from the inside."

By the autumn of 1910, Ruth was increasingly in demand to recite at schools
and private affairs. She must, in her mind, have come to a turning point, a sense
of career beginning, for she purchased an engagement book, a brown-leather-
bound book, gold-tooled borders, initials R. D. in the center. It measured eight
and a half by ten inches and contained blank pages of fine quality white paper.
She wrote the long way of the pages and headed the first one "1910–1911." In
two columns she entered thirty-two engagements for that winter, no dates, only
names: schools, clubs, parties at private homes including those of Mrs. Jacob Schiff,
Mrs. Mortimer Schiff, Mrs. Felix Warburg, Mrs. George Blumenthal, and Mrs.
James Speyer, all patrons of the arts. Ruth now received a fee for her recitals.

The next year, thirty-five engagements were entered; among the fifteen private
parties were those of Mrs. Franklin Roosevelt in Albany (FDR now state sena-
tor); the Groton and Spence Schools; the Princeton Faculty Club; and the Norfolk, Connecticut, fire department.

Dated, more detailed entries began in June 1913 in London. This book holds
the record of her career. It is complete until her later years, when the pace of life
and social demands became too swift for careful notes and one begins to find the
entry, "Some dates lost here." The book ran short of her career so that the last
couple of years are reported on rather casual inserts. On July 2, 1911, Ruth wrote
from Connecticut to her mother's great friend, Mrs. Yates Thompson, in London: "I am doing my monologues professionally. Mother has been much amused
and interested in my experiences. I have had great success." Then she added a long
report on her mother's health:

She has to depend on a heart stimulant most of the time. . . . She leads a perfectly regular life . . . is far from strong and can't stand excitement or any nervous strain. . . . She has a nurse because without one she gets nervous and apprehensive and loses again and feels weak and very ill. She reads and sews and plays solitaire—life is dull. I fear she has little hope within herself. The house [in Maine] is rented; I fear our happy summers there are over.

In October, Alice sailed with Edward and the twins for a two-year assignment in India. Ruth noted, "Mother takes it calmly."

It must have been a worrisome, up-and-down period, but Ruth kept on with her "reciting" in New York and Washington. Mrs. James Roosevelt, Mrs. Harold Pratt, Henry Adams, and other prominent political and social hosts asked her to entertain their guests. On January 7 she attended President Taft's state dinner at the White House for the diplomatic corps and recited afterward. Two months later she sailed to stay with her brother Paul, his wife and son, in London. Paul was studying there, still confident and enthusiastic over his voice, although his mother and Ruth heard varying accounts of his singing.

After their surprise marriage in late March 1909, Paul and Muriel Draper went to Florence for what they came to regard as "two enchanted Italian years." Paul studied with Isidore Bragiotti, a teacher of opera singers. Here young Paul was born, and the fabled and extraordinary Lily Bragiotti took them under her wing.

But Paul sang lieder, and Raimund von Zur Mühlen, the greatest teacher of "lieder" singing, lived in England. So Paul and Muriel and young Paul, in the early summer of 1911, went to England, to Sussex, where von Zur Mühlen took a fancy to Paul and consented to teach him. After eighteen months' work, Paul's voice was becoming what "Master" said it would. Although it was a voice of no great quality, it was a pleasing voice, used with charm and sensitivity in the songs of Brahms, Schumann, and Schubert. Von Zur Mühlen had known Brahms and Clara Schumann and from them learned how this music should be sung.

Paul and Muriel first took a house opposite von Zur Mühlen on Holland Street. Muriel arranged the largest room with a piano, cushions, and all the sofas, and set about filling it with music.

Many have written about Muriel Draper. She is described as slight, with a good figure, tall and graceful. Her head was distinctive with her exotically draped turbans, a jewel suspended on her forehead or an egret feather erect at the front of her headdress. Carl Van Vechten described her features as those of "a white negress." Having fair hair and a fair complexion, she usually wore light colored clothes. Her fine hands were used to great effect in her animated conversation, which was original, penetrating, quick witted, and keenly observant. With great feminine charm, she attracted many male admirers, and, at the same time, she held a large and enduringly devoted group of women friends. Many found her enchanting, though with her loud and Bohemian ways, many did not.

London, in these early years, was visited by many young musical talents, all in their late twenties: Arthur Rubinstein, pianist, the violinists Desirée Defauw, Paul Kochanski, and Albert Sammons with his London String Quartette, the composer Karol Szymanowski. Then there was a group ten years older, already "arrived": Harold Bauer and his sister with their violas, the violinists Jacques Thibaud and Pedro Morales, Pierre Monteux, conductor, Barrere with his flute, and the great cellists, Ernest Schelling, Felix Salmond, Rubio, and, of course, the great musician Pablo Casals, who would outlive them all, becoming a legend in his own time. These would be the outstanding concert performers, the "musical stars," over the next thirty years—brilliant, interesting, individualistic men. It was an extraordinary mix: Spanish, Polish, French, English, and American, with their common nationality in music.

Not daunted by the fact that they had met none of the musicians, Muriel persuaded Paul's manager, Montague Vert Chester, to bring Arthur Rubinstein, then in London for a concert. The dinner was good, the atmosphere congenial—he played. Paul and Muriel attended a concert by Jacques Thibaud, went backstage, presented themselves, and carried him off to Chelsea. Muriel sent a note to Harold Bauer, who came on the word of von Zur Mühlen. Chester brought Pablo Casals, who brought Rubio. Musicians brought other musicians, and thus it became a cosmopolitan gathering uniquely suited to its time and to the making of music for the pure joy of the players. During these three glorious years, almost every musician coming to London was brought to Edith Grove.

The magic was working, the magic of musicians making music with and for musicians, in a house where musical literature was the *lingua franca* and where an artist could relax after a concert, have supper, a nap, and play only if—and what—he desired. They made music far into the morning hours, often until dawn. Rubinstein remembered these nights as "the supreme musical euphoria of my life."

With the acquisition of 19 and 19A Edith Grove—just off the Fulham Road on the far side of Chelsea—Muriel connected the two houses and contrived a larger music room, large enough for them all, even with the occasional addition of Albert Sammons, with his London String Quartette or the Mendelssohn Octet. Rubinstein found them a new piano, a Bechstein.

Soon 17 Edith Grove, adjoining, was purchased and made into two apartments, where Rubinstein and Karol Szymanowski lived. Paul and Zosia Kochanski were just across the street and von Zur Mühlen around the corner.

Norman Douglas, whom Muriel had met at Capri in 1906, lived nearby and became a presence in the house, promising three-year-old Paul a penny for any day he had been really bad and a sound smacking if he had been good. Douglas was the only "listener" except for Henry James, who occasionally came round from Cheyne Walk, watching and absorbing every gesture, expression, and relationship in that room, and John Singer Sargent, who came from Tite Street.

Paul's love of music was the mainspring. After his death, Alice Shurtleff wrote to Ruth. She had been listening to the Philharmonic on the radio, and she said:

"Oh, how much it makes me think of Paul. Forever he is in all music for me. Was there ever anyone who loved it more—who lived it more? When he was a little boy and I wasn't much older, your mother took me to my first concert. I remember they played Tchaikovsky's *Pathetique*. Paul was wild with excitement before and after. Oh, Lord! *Think* of such a spirit at *Groton!*"

This was the milieu into which Ruth Draper stepped in March 1913, and it was here that she formed her great and lasting musical friendships: Ernest Schelling, Arthur Rubinstein, Paul and Zosia Kochanski, Karol Szymanowski, Felix and Helen Salmond, and "Master." Of Russian extraction and German-Baltic upbringing, von Zur Mühlen was an extraordinary character whom Ruth would often visit at his country home, Steyning in Sussex, where he kept his beloved white doves.

Enthralled by the musical nights at Edith Grove, Ruth described them to her mother:

> April 1 [1913], On Sunday night Thibaud, the great French violinist, a Spanish poet, and three other musicians came to dinner. The entire conversation was in French—Paul managed pretty well, I got on all right and of course Muriel is absolutely at home. It was very pleasant and amusing. About 9:30, five or six other musical people came in. After a while a little violinist lady played two short things and then Thibaud, with an excellent cellist and viola played the Brahms A Minor Quartette—too beautiful for words. After that a delicious Mozart string quartette. Then we talked a while and had a little supper, and then Thibaud and Freyer played a Beethoven Sonata; then I recited three monos and Paul sang three songs—extremely well, too— and then we talked and laughed and did stunts and fooled—and suddenly Thibaud sprang to his feet and said: "Je jouais la Chaconne!" which he did and it was sublime—really very, very wonderful. Presently they left and it was five o'clock! It was quite extraordinary— the intensely musical atmosphere. All most natural and easy, no forcing them to play—they wanted to and just went on and on for joy of the music. It was all so cosy and *Gemutlich*.

> May 5 [1913], We have just had a most wonderful evening. Casals, a supreme artist of great charm; Bauer, who played the viola; Rubio, the dear old Spaniard; Goosens, such a nice boy, fiddle; Sous, 1st violin of Sir Henry Wood's orchestra; and Miss Bauer, viola, played the two great Sextettes of Brahms. It was very extraordinary and I shall never forget it. We've all just had scrambled eggs (which Paul always makes on a chafing dish to perfection), milk, bread and butter, a bottle of champagne for the exhausted artists, coffee and cut fruit. This is the usual musical supper and *so* good! Now they have all gone back to the studio and Casals and another Spaniard are playing and sing-

ing old Spanish folk-songs and lullabys. It sounds too enchanting
coming up the studio stairs. I think of you all the time with this music,
it is so beautiful and I'm so glad you taught us to love it. Paul speaks
of you constantly and the pleasure you would have in hearing it.

Ruth's ripening friendships in the arts were not limited to the music world.
Literature also offered attachments.

Friendship between the Dana and James families had begun with Charles A.
Dana and Henry James Sr. and was well established by Ruth's generation, Henry
Jr. being a friend of her mother's. So, when Ruth arrived in London in 1913 to
visit Paul, she sent a note to Henry James asking if she might call. In a letter to
her mother she wrote:

> March 1st was a memorable afternoon. I went to see Mr. James at three
> and had a delightful talk with him and at four got up to go—he said
> he was going out and offered to drop me anywhere. Then he found
> a lot of things he had to get for the flat, and I said I was too early for
> tea and I'd go and shop with him. So we first went to the Atheneum
> Club and got some money and then we went to The [Army and Navy]
> Stores and bought an icebox, a kitchen scale, prunes, a wall brush and
> three teapots and a clock. We had a lovely time and then he brought
> me to Mrs. Rathbone's door. *Really* it was too funny for words. I think
> I helped him in choosing and at any rate enjoyed myself enormously
> and have stored up a most delightful memory.
>
> Young Paul constantly hears his mother speak of Mr. James and
> when he was shown Henry James's new book he liked the title, *A
> Small Boy and Others*, with the picture of H. J. as a child, and last
> night went to sleep with his arms around the book. H. J. was delighted
> when I told him today.

He wanted to see the boy, but when Paul eagerly rushed into the room to be
met by Henry James's rumblings and huffings in search of the precise word to
convey his meaning, and explosive triumph when he did, the four-year-old child
was so frightened that he fled the room.

H.R.H. Princess Christian of Schleswig-Holstein (Princess Helena, third daughter of Queen Victoria) asked Ruth to recite at a small private party and, again, at
a second party. Then on May 8, Ruth wrote to her mother:

> Lord Sandhurst telephoned to say the Queen [Queen Mary] wanted
> to hear me and would go to tea with Princess Christian on the 16th.
> Paul was so thrilled he insisted on cabling. Of course, I still fear the
> [Princess] may die, but if not, I shall have the great honor! I feel I must
> get a new dress as I've already worn my red to Pcss. C. and it's rather
> dark and *defraiché*, and my friends [in Paris] insist on my going to

Worth. He is to choose the color and stuff and *façon* and I shall have little to say! He has been told that I am a professional and that the dress is to appear before the Queen, so he is much interested and will attend to it himself. Uncle Henry [Adams] is much excited.

Ruth had just arrived in Paris when she wrote to Dorothea:

I walked with Uncle Henry thro' the Bois and Bagatelle, which I'd never seen, and the flowers and green were too exquisite. This afternoon I ordered a dress at "Worth's"! I've no idea yet what it will be. I hope it will be pretty. Mr. Worth is to decide tomorrow at 11 and I feel as if I were going to a medical specialist—that same squeamish feeling. I shan't dare or offer any suggestions.

This season was the genesis of Ruth's entry into London society and her considerable social success. This was her own achievement. Her talent in combination with her individual grace and quality of person appealed to a London society that was interested that a young woman of her obvious background should pursue a stage career and yet remain so firmly within her own milieu and dignity.

To her mother, Ruth later wrote: "I've got the prettiest hat you ever saw—useless and expensive! Paul is so glad to see me at last do something rash—he almost cabled you! I know Doro will be delighted."

On May 17 Ruth sat for John Singer Sargent, whom she had asked to draw her portrait as a present to her mother (who already had Sargent's handsome drawing of Dr. Draper). The drawing shows a quiet young woman with beautiful eyes, a shirred ruffle at her throat, reserved, dignified, and stylish. A few evenings later, Sargent stood at the Yates Thompson's, watching for the first time as Ruth performed her monologues. The next morning he wrote begging her to destroy the drawing—it was *non avenu*—he had not "seen" her at all. He asked her to sit for him again, but as she was shortly to sail for home, she promised to do so the next year. She took the drawing with her.

Also on the 17th, Ruth lunched with Henry James, writing her mother that "he was very sweet and sympathetic through all my indecision." By this time she regarded him as the friend and counselor to whom she could turn with the baffling problem of her future: Should she develop her dramatic talent or pursue her poetic ambitions as a writer? H. J. made his variously quoted reply, here given as Ruth dictated it many years later to Neville Rogers: "My dear young friend—my dear young friend—you have made—my dear young friend you have woven—my dear young friend you have woven yourself a magic carpet—stand on it!" And Neville Rogers said that in telling of the conversation, Ruth Draper assumed all the expressions and mannerisms of Henry James—uncannily "like."

It is in these letters of 1913, from London, that Ruth's handwriting took shape—firm, fluent, quickly paced, without error or change of word—the handwriting in which, over next forty-four years, she would build her lines of communication to family, friends of long standing, and a varied and steadily enlarging roster of new friends and acquaintances. Her letters must have numbered in the tens of thousands, some of poignant beauty, many of topical interest, the greater number merely of trivia or family chat, arrangements about this or that—always there was something that must be done for someone else.

Henry James wrote a "piece" for Ruth Draper to perform. On December 4, 1913, from 21, Carlyle Mansions, Cheyne Walk, London SW, he sent a letter to her—a long Henry James letter—to say that the MS of the play had been posted. He could not see why it would not go, he could see her in it, and, although offering numerous suggestions, he would, of course, leave its interpretation to her genius. He insisted that no public mention be made of his authorship. Its authorship, however, was unmistakable! Ruth never attempted a performance: The character was not congenial to her talents, and Henry James's words did not come easily from her lips. With the utmost tact, she returned the "piece" to him. He must have been disappointed in this, his last attempt to create a Henry James presence in the theatre in his lifetime.

In November, in her strong indomitable hand, Mrs. Draper wrote to John Jay Chapman in admiration of his biography of Albert Gallatin and telling him of the engagement of her daughter Dorothea to Linzee Blagden. She asked him to call to chat with her—after the wedding.

Early in December Ruth wrote again to Mrs. Yates Thompson: "Mother is very ill and slowly growing weaker ever since the end of October. An extraordinary vitality on both sides of the family persists in her and the fight may yet be long."

Extraordinary woman that she was, Mrs. Draper's humor and turns of mind and phrase can be illuminated only by one of her own letters. Written on January 7, 1914, to "Jane," as Ruth was known to her immediate family, though why no one now remembers:

> I was very glad to have your letter. I shall never live down the habit of so many years, of considering you as my little child, and it is always an anxious moment that mounts you into a Pullman car for a night journey. Forth into the black night you go, far, where the antennae of my heart are powerless to act as a safety cord, and I have to just drop you into the chasms measureless to man, and hope that you will get out safe in the morning.
>
> I have just finished the pink embroidery on the blankets. That makes four—big monograms so badly done that it is wrong to add such a lot to the great failure collection. But as you know, I am of that happy, industrious kind "never weary of ill doing" and I pick up the dropped stitches of perfection and cheerfully drop them again! And continue to stub my toe against my blunders.
>
> . . . My sweet little cold is clearing up nicely. Yesterday I had a fever. That reminds me—I have now put in the thermometer. I'll re-

port in a minute. I have had the account from the Treasurer of the Alley Fund, asking for my usual $100. I have sent $50, promising $50 in three months. I had a little money slyly put by, but there is always a Pirate lurking to get such wealth away from me. I shall be delighted to get you back. (I have no fever).

Good-bye, love. Ever fondly, Ma

On January 24, Ruth wrote Corinne Robinson, niece of Theodore Roosevelt and her close childhood friend: "I don't lunch out much and am listless about asking anyone here. I really don't want them, to be frank. I seem to care less for everyone; they bore me, I suppose, but I feel my heart is hard and I only love one person in the world and God chooses to take her painfully and slowly from me." At the same time, Ruth was giving thought to her monologues, for she added: "I must go on with this thing for I am trying to take it seriously and consider it a profession."

June 1914 found Ruth again in London, undertaking eleven private engagements as her reputation and popularity grew. Her talent was an appropriate asset on many occasions.

She saw Henry James frequently and again sat to John Singer Sargent in his studio at 31 Tite Street, which formerly had been Whistler's studio (then numbered 13 Title Street). In this high-ceilinged studio overlooking a green Chelsea garden, Ruth accompanied Henry James for many hours of *his* sittings, chatting to keep his expression lively. It is amusing to think of Ruth and H. J. happily chatting in this studio where hung Sargent's portrait of Madame X (Mme. Gutreau)—now hanging in the American Wing of New York's Metropolitan Museum of Art—which caused such an uproar at the Paris Salon of 1884 that it may well have been a contributing reason for Sargent to leave Paris and to establish his studio in London. This studio, so steeped in the history of Whistler's years, is where Sargent painted his great portrait of Ellen Terry as Lady Macbeth, for which, in full costume, she would descend from a four-wheeler, carefully observed by Oscar Wilde from behind the curtain in his house across the street.

In her own sitting of less than two hours, Sargent accomplished two brilliant charcoal drawings of Ruth Draper in character: *A Dalmatian Peasant in the Hall of a New York Hospital*—"rather grim and unpleasant but as I look, I am sure"—and as Lesley McGregor, *The Scottish Immigrant*. This became her distinctive poster for her entire professional career. "And, my dear, he wouldn't take a cent for them, not a cent!" (The portraits are now in the Theatre Collection of the Museum of the City of New York).

This was the last glorious prewar London season. The opera and concerts were brilliant—Chaliapin sang Boris Godunov—and Sergei Diaghilev brought his Russian Ballet. There was, however, no musical party at Edith Grove after Pierre Monteux conducted *Le Sacre de Printemps* at Drury Lane. Muriel and Paul were in the audience with Rubinstein, Szymanowski, and the Kochanskis. Muriel was too stunned even to discuss the sensational music and historic performance. Ruth was in London, but there is no indication that she attended. Muriel, however, made sure that Nijinsky and Monteux came to Edith Grove, as well as Chaliapin. She promptly came to know Diaghilev and sat in the stalls with him at rehearsal.

For Paul and Muriel, however, it was a disastrous summer. Nothing was ever to be the same again—as it was not for anyone in England after August 4—but Paul's disaster was of his own making and happened at the Derby in June.

Paul had been courting catastrophe for some time. Besides his periodic drinking bouts, he was an inveterate gambler. Usually lucky, and winning handsomely on an Irish Sweepstake, he had financed the music lessons, Edith Grove, the box parties, and the Savoy Grill suppers, but his luck ran out, and he was in debt, most heavily to his bookmaker. He bet all he had left on the Derby—and lost; every penny suddenly and irretrievably vanished. As a mortgage on the house failed to meet his debts, Ruth provided some crucial help, though her resources, borrowed from Ba (Ruth's eldest half sister, Martha, known in the family as Ba, or Barie), were limited. She sailed early in July in the *Lusitania* to New York.

Without regard to the gathering war clouds, Paul decided to go to Germany to sing to German audiences the Schumann "Winterreisse" and their own lieder. He left London the last week in July, and nothing was heard of him until he reappeared in London in September.

At two minutes past eight o'clock on the morning of August 4, the German Army invaded Belgium. War had begun. The evening before, Sir Edward Grey, England's foreign secretary, spoke words that would forever echo in the minds of all those then old enough to understand: "The lamps are going out all over Europe; we shall not see them lit again in our lifetime."

Many people thought the war would be over by Christmas. They called it the war to end war and it would go on for four years.

On Sunday, August 16, Ruth wrote from Mt. Kisco, from Will Draper's house, to Alice in India: "It is now half past five, a lovely soft afternoon and Ba and I are alone. Mother died quietly this morning at half past three. . . . The stroke was appallingly sudden. . . . It would have killed me to be away from her. With all my selfishness and often disregard, my love was very intense and our companionship most close and tender. . . . Her influence and inspiration to me will always be fixed in my mind with adoration and gratitude. She was always loathe that we should lose anything from life on account of her." Mrs. Draper was a few months past her sixty-fourth birthday.

No longer was there a focal point for the family. Ruth was free to explore, to find her fulfillment in a world being shaken to its foundations. Her own foundation held firm, solid as New England rock, on which to build her self and her career. Proceeding cautiously, she seemed to have a sure instinct for what she must do, step by step, one step at a time.

3

Exploration

NOT YET, HOWEVER, WAS RUTH TOTALLY free; the family patterns could not so quickly be broken.

Will, George, Dorothea, and Alice were married. Paul had returned from London because of his mother's death. The war continued, but Muriel, with the children, would stick it out on credit until the following May. Ruth and Charles and Martha remained at home; they sold the big house on 8th Street, and Ruth settled them all at 125 East 36th Street. But she "felt very strongly that [she] must go on with [her] work and find new fields among strangers."

So, on January 18, taking her mother's old Scottish maid, Christine, she set forth—without agent or manager or prior bookings. She went to Pittsburgh, Cincinnati, Chicago, St. Louis, and Kansas City, to Colorado Springs, to Pasadena, Santa Barbara, and on up the West Coast to Seattle and Vancouver. In some cities she had friends, or introductions; in others she wrote ahead to the manager of the best hotel, asking if she might give a recital for the hotel guests and the public. In Denver, the hotel manager was

> not encouraging about a recital there unless I am on hand to arrange the details—so I won't go! I do not plan any more "on my own"; the fuss of attending to it all is more than it is worth. Private affairs have certainly spoiled me—$150. safe and no fuss or worry. It is very unambitious of me, but I'll wait until I fail [in private bookings] first.

From Pittsburgh, her first stop, Ruth wrote to Dorothea, "I had great success yesterday and the enthusiasm augurs well for Western audiences." At the end of her tour, Ruth wrote to Mrs. Yates Thompson, "I have had really wonderful luck considering I knew practically no one to start with and it was only by word being passed along that I secured engagements and ventured to give a few on my own." In five months and eighteen cities across the United States, she gave forty recitals. "I made $4813.46 and the whole trip, including Christine and a new hat (with some added to be on the outside) cost $1420."

In this way, Ruth began to explore the dimensions of a professional career. Setting forth from her protected New York social world, this was the first of many tours that would continue throughout her professional career. Perhaps it was her innocence, her almost childlike trustfulness, her matter-of-fact self-confidence that protected her "on the road." Perhaps it was a native New England shrewdness. Without experience, Ruth seems to have known exactly what she would and would not accept—which says a good deal for established standards of conduct.

With this reliance upon her independent judgment, Ruth conducted her long career over the next forty-two years. In time, there would be agents and managers and professionalism, but basically her attitude remained the same. As her success grew, as the theatres would be "sold out and hundreds turned away"—often in the United States and almost always in Great Britain and in Europe—she would shake her head, incredulous and amazed, pleased but a little apprehensive about living up to it all. "Isn't it ridiculous!" she would say. In all the years to come, on tour after tour, she would write, as she did in 1928: "The enthusiasm is great—I could get more work if I could stay longer. People are very urgent and can't understand my leaving. Many want to hear me again. They think I am crazy to leave."

At this point, it should be remembered that across the United States in the eighteenth and nineteenth centuries, the theatre had to make its way in the face of inherited Puritan morality and American Victorian prejudice—a prejudice stemming from the conviction of Pilgrim ancestors that the theatre was a place of sin and wickedness, populated by disreputable people. Even attendance at the theatre was frowned upon, except in a center like New York, where culture was developing and the shackles of prejudice were broken somewhat earlier. Only by the early twentieth century was attendance more generally acceptable.

As for appearance *on* the stage—"to appear before the public, for money!" that was something no "nice girl" of a respectable family could possibly even consider and hope to retain her reputation for virtue. Any woman appearing on the stage was promptly branded "an actress!" whose moral character was clearly in question. However, the growth of platform readings by women of unimpeachable reputation brought some respectability, and World War I would, for all practical purposes, effectively end American Victorian prejudice, except in the more conservative enclaves.

Shy and reserved as Ruth was, there were moments on this tour of starry-eyed emotion. In Santa Barbara she met "an elderly Southern gentleman, much traveled, with great charm and full of thoughts and imagination." Quite by chance they met again in San Francisco in the lobby of the St. Francis Hotel. He asked her to go to Yosemite with him at the end of May. She wrote to Dorothea: "He's taking a niece and great niece, so I'm not so tempted as I might be. I glowed with pleasure at seeing him—he's adorable; you know that heavenly feeling of knowing all your charm is concentrated and iridescent, coming *out* of you for just a few priceless minutes. Well, I had that rare feeling for two minutes. I know I was beautiful, glowing and fascinating in his eyes—and then we parted. Poor old soul, he's off alone. He touched me and made me realize how precious and fine is the sudden touch of kindred souls. . . . I value highly finding him and his instant finding of me." And she added, "This is private—don't laugh and read it to the others."

"The atmosphere here is full of War," Ruth wrote from Vancouver on May 10, where everyone was shocked by the submarine sinking of the passenger ship *Lusitania*. Many Americans were aboard. "The feeling against the U.S. Government is *very* bitter. Apparently they all think we should be in it and are anxiously awaiting our attitude about the *Lusitania* horror. I confess I am too. I don't see how we can stand by and see such an outrage."

Ruth returned East to a summer tour of the Maine Coast resorts and benefits for war charities: French hospitals, Polish fete with Paderewski, Serbian nurses, American Ambulance Service, Belgian Milk Fund, Canadian Hospitals Fund, the Red Cross, as well as the home needs of district nurses. She went on a sixteen-stop tour with Elizabeth Perkins in October 1916 to benefit the American Fund for the French Wounded. Appearances at private parties continued. She and Lizzie knit twenty pairs of socks.

On October 17, 1915, Ruth performed on a stage for the first time. The Neighborhood Playhouse on 466 Grand Street in New York presented Paul Draper singing German lieder; Ruth Draper in five monologues; and Albert J. Carroll and the Chalif Dancers in a Pierrot Dance. These five monologues, interesting to note, would remain in Ruth's repertory throughout her career, albeit with many refinements. They were *A Southern Girl at a Dance*, *A Class in Greek Poise*, *A Dalmatian Peasant in the Hall of a New York Hospital*, *Three Generations in a Court of Domestic Relations*, and *The Scottish Immigrant*.

Still she remained unsure of her direction. Clearly it was the theatre; repeatedly she heard: "Really, Ruth, you *must* go on the stage!" But *which* stage? In what guise? In her own production, in her own creation, entirely alone? With other players, in a stage play, written and produced by someone else? How could she be sure?

Although Henry James had advised Ruth to stand on her own magic carpet, she had gone to see Charles Frohman, the great American theatrical producer and a noted developer of talent. He said: "You have a unique and original gift; keep to your own form of drama. Do *not* act in stage plays." Still she was not convinced and attempted two further experiments. In May of 1916 she canceled twelve scheduled engagements to undertake the part of the lady's maid in Cyril Harcourt's *A Lady's Name*—a very small part. Marie Tempest was the star, with Daisy Belmore and Beyrl Mercer. It ran a total of six weeks. The critics found nothing to say about Ruth's performance.

The next February (1917), for a single performance, Ruth staged and performed in her own production of Strindberg's *The Stronger*. A pantomime of her own devising followed, and then she performed her own character drama, *The Actress*, which would become one of the most brilliant and popular monologues in her repertoire. Only *The Actress* received good notices; the program as a whole was damned as "ill-advised, misguided and tedious."

At last she was persuaded and did not again attempt a part in a stage play with other actors or in a work that she herself had not written. There were, of course, various charity events that she supported by appearing with a stellar group, but they were few.

In April of 1917, at the old Hippodrome on Madison Square, Ruth performed her monologue *Vive la France—1916*, a short, dramatic highly charged showstopper. In it she portrayed a French woman searching for news of her husband among the retreating troops, only to learn that he had been killed. Holding her baby above her head, she shouts "Vive la France! Vive la France!"

The United States entered the war on April 6, 1917. For a year Ruth visited army camps and hospitals and gave benefit performances. She raised $10,600 for the Red Cross in a three-week thirty-three stop tour. But this was not enough. Her brothers were in uniform. Her sister-in-law Helen Hoffman Draper and sister Martha Draper were carrying out assignments in France for the Red Cross. Malvina Hoffman also was in Red Cross uniform. Ruth's first cousin Janet Dana trained as a nurse in 1914 and served for a year at the front with the French army, and at Dunkirk; Dorothea had trained with her but remained in the United States. Ruth knew that she must play some part in the reality of the war and found a job at the International Arms and Fuse Factory in Bloomfield, New Jersey.

On June 22, 1918, she wrote Laura White describing the experience, for her so totally new. Ruth found great satisfaction in working the levers that drilled a small bronze knob into a percussion cap. Already she had turned out seventeen thousand. As usual, she was observant and thoughtful of the people around her. "I find the whole experience enormously interesting."

Work from 7:00 in the morning until after 5:00 in the afternoon, lunging at levers, eyes fixed on a whirling cylinder, left her too tired for much more than "tumble into bed by 8:30," after supper and a glance at the papers. "One wonders how these young creatures who've known nothing else but work, can get any of the richness and beauty of life—I suppose they take some time from the night—and find it in the movies and the street! Really we are mad! to see youth—there are some lovely girls—shut up all these perfect days—straining their bodies, producing things to kill people with—one gasps at the insanity of it all. But I'm so thankful I am here!" She signed herself "Drill Hand No. 20921."

After two months at the Fuse Factory, Ruth received an assignment from the YMCA to entertain American troops overseas, and on October 12, 1918, she embarked on the SS *Baltic* for a voyage of twelve days in convoy. On board, the first night, she wrote to Dorothea: "I've not found your letter yet, but know it will be a comfort to me tonight! Think of me always as loving, admiring and thankful for your tenderness, your support of my frail purpose, and your understanding. . . . If anything happens to me—think of me as unafraid and asking nothing more of life. I only hope that I can be of service over there, and come back with more to give here!" She added, "I've already been addressed by a cheerful 'Y' secretary and given him the frozen face! I must get the 'Y' spirit."

The *Baltic* was the lead ship in what was said to be the largest all-troop convoy of the war—17,500 men; it was escorted by U.S. Navy destroyers on the first half of the voyage and by British navy destroyers for the remainder. Mrs. Harold Pratt was just down the corridor. "She and a charming English girl and I have great fun;

I should be badly off without them for female companionship." By the merest chance, sixty-one years later, this biographer met the "charming English girl," then Mrs. Gordon H. Michler and living in Connecticut. Herself very shy, she felt she had not really got to know Ruth Draper, who seemed to her very much as Aileen Tone described her at twelve—"grave and simple and observant." There was another "reciter—she does plays and monologues and has been to Schools of Expression and is a perfect type to make a monologue [for me]. I fear I am right in thinking she is not the right stuff, but like me, she can probably swing into canteen work if she doesn't please." These four were the only women aboard. Mrs. Pratt was surely the dominant personality, and her presence understandably gave Ruth a sense of security. "Various Naval and Army officers keep us extremely busy and, besides, I am teaching French classes; a morning one for N.C.O's and an evening one for officers." She was surprised to find "so many comforts, everything clean and the food sufficient. No hardships whatever." Ruth was interested in all the people aboard and troubled by the attitudes of the men. She wrote:

> The U.S. and British officers, and the N.C.O.s of both countries, might as well be enemies—they never speak to each other. There is a bunch of Japs—very distinguished looking little men, a Minister to Switzerland and Sweden, I think among them. There is also a lonely Belgian officer and a loyal Hindu from Harvard going back to fight for England, and no one speaks to them. Brotherly love is no more evident than before, even on the brink of Eternity, when it is expressed in terms of social intercourse!
>
> We have drill everyday and are not allowed to move without our [life] belts, but otherwise one is free from consciousness of the danger, though one idly chats and speculates about it. Our feelings will no doubt be different from now on . . . tonight we enter the danger zone.

The ship docked safely in Liverpool late on Thursday afternoon, October 24, after what may have been the most perilous part of the journey; the boom protecting the harbor at night had been dropped just before the convoy arrived, and the ships were spread out all night, like sitting ducks, while all on board slept in their life belts. Arriving in London the next morning, Ruth immediately reported at YMCA headquarters and then hurried to Oxford to see her sister Alice and the Carter's four children. "The twins speak charmingly. Alice is more American than ever."

In London, Ruth recited at officers clubs, Red Cross huts, and small hospitals. Because of the influenza epidemic (that worldwide epidemic that took more lives than were lost in the four years of the war), visitors were not permitted at the big military hospitals. "The sight of the wounded and blind stabs me to the heart and I find the tears very near." She saw her English friends and many men friends from New York and "sat with Hoyty Wiborg who has been quite ill after a flu *picure*. She is full of her experiences and is here for a rest, dancing every night." (Hoyty had done grueling and heroic work at a forward medical station). The three strikingly beautiful Wiborg sisters, introduced to London society by Lady Diana Manners (later married to Duff Cooper), became "the rage of London," singing American folk songs in three-part harmony to the delight of European listeners. Her sister Sara married Gerald Murphy and became part of the legendary 1920s in Paris and on the Riviera.

Edward Carter, in England for his first visit since August, was suddenly called back to Paris; he asked Ruth to accompany him. But Ruth "was so slow moving, it never occurred to [her] to change [her] plans." So she missed an opportunity to be at the front when the last barrage was fired and the Armistice became effective, at 11:00 A.M. on November 11, 1918. "I don't think I'll ever get over it!" Ruth and Alice were in London but "didn't think" to go near Buckingham Palace, the focal point of the cheering.

Ruth sought impressions of every significant event. Feeling intensely and responding always with deep emotion, her wartime experiences surely contributed to her seemingly inexhaustible understanding of human emotion. She wrote from Paris on the 14th to Martha Draper:

> Here I am. That should be enough for you to know just what I am feeling, thinking and seeing! I came across, through *le Havre*, with Mrs. Whitelaw Reid and she was so kind and friendly. The weather is perfect and late yesterday afternoon I strolled at once to the *Place de la Concorde* and the sky was all pink and a lovely moon was straight over the *Tuileries* Garden. The *Place* filled with guns, captured aeroplanes all along the balustrade of the *Tuileries*; dozens of children climbing and tumbling over the guns—swinging on them—laughing and shouting. *Mme. Strasbourg* [the statue which had been draped in black since Alsace had been annexed by Germany during the Franco-Prussian War of 1871] was a mass of flowers and the mob was thick about her. The crowd of quiet, slowly moving men and women marvelous . . . groups of girls and "*poilus*" were gay in their expression but, though faces were smiling, there was a most moving silence in the crowd.
>
> Why is it flags seem to fly more wonderfully in Paris than anywhere else? I bought some hot chestnuts on the *Faubourg St. Honore* and ate them in the side streets. I walked about until dark stifled with emotion.

With Aileen Tone and Mrs. Pratt, Ruth went to Notre Dame to the great service of Thanksgiving. "The church was full of light, owing to the glass in the transept windows being removed, so that all the beauty of the stone and architecture came into evidence. Flags everywhere, as only the French seem to know how to mass and drape them. . . . The great bell, silent since the war, was booming and sent shivers through one, and when the organ pealed out in a triumphant march I almost blew up. There was a fanfare of trumpets now and then and the whole crowd joined in singing the Te Deum and the Magnificat."

Many of her New York and Boston friends were in Paris at this time and many

English friends too, for all through this War there had been much to-ing and fro-ing between London and Paris. Janetta Alexander, working with the Red Cross, and Arnold Whitridge were there, and their marriage touched her romantic heart. They were old friends—some of her earliest recitals were given in the Whitridge house near Washington Square. It was in November that Arnold had met Janetta at a dinner party at *La Rue*, given by his Groton and Yale classmate, Cole Porter. Immediately he had said, "That is the girl I am going to marry!" He returned to his artillery unit at the front, they corresponded, he proposed, and in April 1918 obtained a four-day leave. At the *Mairie* in Paris they were married, although the mayor was so taken with Edith Wharton, one of Arnold's witnesses, that Janetta feared he might make Mrs. Wharton the bride. After a two-day honeymoon in Fontainebleau, they did not meet again until after the Armistice. At the reception that followed their church wedding in the American Cathedral, Ruth gave them a recital.

Young and of such limited experience, Ruth could not accept the average, hardworking, not very attractive YMCA workers whose "good-cheer smile withered [her] soul." This was not really snobbery but more a lack of understanding—she just wanted them to be less dull. Notably kind, compassionate, and generous wherever she saw need, Ruth was not one to take up the banner for a "cause": honesty, compassion, pity, kindness as a way of life, but not as a "cause."

Anxious "to get away to a stiffer job," Ruth found it almost more than she could bear "to be one of the (apparently) idle women in uniform. One feels so *de trop* and so American and like clearing out immediately. Everyone is puzzled whether to leave or stay and all the men think about is getting home. It is very curious, this indifference as to what is going to be the outcome of the [Peace] Conference. . . . The breaking down of morale is very evident."

She heard Edward Carter "make an address to a group of [YMCA] workers starting off to the field. It was really *very fine*." A grudging comment, this, because the character and value of Edward's work was not understood by his sisters-in-law. Edward Carter was a very able man committed to working for the betterment of conditions and people, no matter what their religious, political, or social position. Neither he nor Alice found "society" as such to be worth while. At this period, Ruth's letters to Dorothea are full of dismay at the way of life imposed upon Alice because of Edward's work: The Carters had less money, and Alice had none of the pleasures, as her sisters counted pleasures; she seemed to them to be oblivious to a standard of living that they considered important; that Alice's impending move to Paris would be the twenty-ninth move in the ten years since her marriage was more than they could accept. "I wish Ma and Pa and Grandpa were here to remind her who she is," wrote Ruth. "Y-ism is a blight. Oh, I *am* so wicked." She added, "I don't mean this in an arrogant way but she necessarily associates with such small people." With this point of view, there was no possibility that Ruth could understand Edward's work. What they wanted for Alice, however, was not necessarily what Alice wanted—or needed. The gift of a black velvet and lace tea gown, intended to raise Alice's spirits, did, at least by the giving, somewhat comfort Ruth. She gave Edward "some very frank talk in Paris. I think it did some good."

Socially, Ruth had an interesting time. She had tea with Edith Wharton and dined with Aileen Tone, "Hoyty" Wiborg, and with Elizabeth Hoyt, where Edie Hoyt came and General Pershing.

> It was very cosy and pleasant and really amusing to see him with we three undazzling young women. Elizabeth is, of course, very funny and has such poise and ease and he might have been Uncle John, for all the excitement he caused. We just chatted and talked pleasantly and laughed a good deal 'til he left for his train. He and Elizabeth went into another room for a few moments to discuss a Red Cross trip she is about to take, and maybe other things, but I could see no particular evidence of devotion, he just seemed to enjoy her and the restful evening. He asked me to surely come to Hq. when I come to Chaumont and spoke most admiringly of Edward and claimed to remember Paul's gracious delivery of his speech at Blois. I like him very much in spite of certain prejudices due to stories I'd heard.

At last Ruth joined her YMCA colleague, Harriet Marple of Bexley, Ohio, five years younger than Ruth, strong, vital, handsome, decisive, and very stylish. Only five feet in height—to Ruth's five feet four inches—she was a small dynamo. They became devoted friends, their natural congeniality intensified by their shared wartime experiences. Both were romantic, fun loving, and searching for their niche in life—and independence—although each was longing for a knight on a white horse. For the next ten months, they would, of necessity, become inseparable companions. More than anyone else, Harriet would come to know Ruth's hopes and fears, her anxieties and dreams—all that Ruth's sisters were never to know— of the agonies and involvement's of her heart. Only Aileen Tone appears to have been on an equal level of intimacy.

Ruth thoroughly enjoyed their assignments at the American Expeditionary Force (AEF) rest camps. Between November and February, she recited nearly a hundred times, working "almost entirely among men who've fought; the few groups who haven't been through it are markedly different, tho' it's hard to tell how." Each group varied in background, and she was "amazed the way the old [monologues] go. . . . The city men are the least appreciative and keen, but I've had some evenings that have me marching in the clouds." More than once she stood on two tables in a shell-torn house, with the only light three candles at her feet. Often they performed two and three times a day, and there were many long cold drives with uncertain cars and equally uncertain drivers. She worked in Neuchateau, Nancy, Chaumont, Semur, and Montigny-sur-Aube, Aignay-le-duc, Tonnerre.

Ruth rode in the mornings with a nice French lieutenant and walked in the moonlight with a nicer American lieutenant and lunched with a charming officer from North Carolina. She fell deeply in love.

"I am enjoying this wandering life," she reassured Dorothea. And to Adolph

Borie she wrote: "I don't think I'll ever come home. I'm so happy over here." By December, Ruth was preparing the ground for her effective independence. She wrote Dorothea that she was considering a return journey eastward around the world. "I may never get another chance," she said. And she asked that Dorothea tell Ba that "Ba must not count on me for a joint abode in the near future." She wondered if Ba had any plans to settle for herself. "It will have to be discussed sooner or later—I dread it."

Ruth performed for the British Peace Delegates at a party in the Hotel Majestic arranged by Lionel Curtis (of Milner's Round Table), now on the League of Nations Commission, and "lunched there with a young Colonel Lawrence who organized the Arab army. A thrilling adventurer with the eyes of Cardinal Newman."

Her war service ended on August 1, 1919. Her experiences during the five years since the death of her mother had been, essentially, exploration, a time of maturing. She now realized that she must remain uncommitted, except to her own talent. Her work with the troops had a general appeal. She had appeared before men of all ages and a diversity of backgrounds, education, and attitudes. The experience had taken her out of the drawing room and placed her squarely before the public. She was now thirty-five years old; it was time to make up her mind.

With Harriet, Ruth took a bicycle trip in Ireland, where she encountered an old Irish woman who told of her grief for her son, killed in the war, until he came to her one night, saying, "Give over weeping, now, Mother, or my wounds will never heal." This is the only identifiable character in her entire repertoire.

Harriet sailed for home, and Ruth settled down in London in a comfortable lodging at 122 Ebury Street. In November she recited at eight private parties of Edwardian hostesses, among them Mrs. George Keppel, the witty, totally discreet Alice, the perfect royal mistress of Edward VII's last years, and Margot Asquith, wife of the prime minister, noted for her sharp wit and acid tongue. Ruth would repeat these visits as she would also the parties of Lord and Lady Curzon, he the foreign minister and former Viceroy of India, on the occasion of their entertaining the King and Queen of Spain. Ruth attracted King Alfonzo's admiring attention.

She spent $223 for a dress by Worth. RUTH DRAPER booked Æolian Hall in London for one matinee on January 29, 1920.

This would be her professional debut on the stage of a legitimate theatre. Step by cautious step she had arrived, the months and years between steps providing time for growth, for adjustment, for appraisal. Her decision now made, independently, at her own risk and in her own time—her career began. It had been a long adolescence.

4

The Drapers after World War I

THE DRAPERS, THE IMMEDIATE FAMILY UNIT of four brothers and four sisters, were the basic reality of Ruth Draper's life. She knew herself as part of this solid structure. Her parents and grandparents—the ones who had gone before—were ever in her mind, and she often would speak of her "cloud of witnesses" on whom she called before stepping onto the stage or before any great occasion in her life; she felt them constantly about her.

Ruth Draper lived her life on three levels: the level of her family, that of her friends, and, the grid on which all else was plotted, that of her work. To some extent, each level overlay the others—a navigational nightmare had it not been that her polestar was her work, all other considerations being weighed against her professional career.

While her monologues—her "work"—came first, the family was the context against which she must be "read." She was part of them and they of her, and, wittingly or not, she must have received some influence from their lives. Clearly, their lives affected her emotionally and occupied her thoughts.

It would be well to take a brief look at these lives in the early 1920s, for the Drapers were very different, one from another. They were self-centered, individualistic, independent, and they knew their own strong-willed minds. Yet, with all their diversity, they conformed to a standard of behavior, of dignity and rectitude. It remained for Ruth, however, to set her own standard of independent purpose and action, but with the utmost correctness and propriety.

Alice Olin Draper had a quiet depth of understanding, a gentle strength, a subtlety of force, dignified, erect, even stately. With her perceptive kindliness, Alice was a person one could approach with trust, with a certainty of sympathy, for, like Charles, Alice listened. She became the most experienced on the basic level of humanity, the one most familiar with the realities of everyday life, which seemed to reinforce her sweetness and simplicity. Alice could be very impressive, but she took care to play a supporting role to Edward's lead.

The drummer to which Alice marched was not heard by Ruth or by Dorothea. She had graduated from Barnard College, and she meant her education to be put to some purpose. The usual pursuits of her contemporaries did not interest her.

Although Dorothea and Janet Dana, her first cousin, without college educations, were setting a course toward more than a "society" life, Alice's view ranged wider.

Edward, when Alice first met him at a religious conference at Barnard, already had spent six years in Calcutta as national secretary of the YMCA of India. Intense, purposeful, not a proselytizer, but committed to a career with a view on the world's people, he was calm, sure of himself, and he knew exactly what he wished to do with his life. With his tall, handsome, rugged maleness, Edward interested Alice, for he presented a dimension entirely new to her. There must have been surprises and adjustments to be made, but this was the way she chose, and she was steadfast in her living.

The son of a congregational minister in Massachusetts, Edward had attended Phillips Academy, in Andover, and Harvard College. After their marriage in August 1908, Alice and Edward spent three years in the United States, where he was secretary of the North American Student Movement, and where their twin sons were born in 1909. Then Edward was called back to Calcutta for another five years as national secretary of the YMCA, for he had a particular genius of understanding and effective, constructive dealing with the people of many countries. "Carter's vision is always two years ahead of the field and he sees into India as into a clear glass," said a member of the Indian government, as quoted by Katherine Mayo in her book *That Damn Y*. The British civil government gave him entire confidence and the burden of welfare work. Not one for theories, what Edward offered was friendship and service. Ultimately, he received the government's highest civilian award—a gold medal, the Kaiser-i-hind. It was a source of regret that his extraordinarily sympathetic understanding of India's needs could not be used at the highest levels of British government. Ruth might have learned much from Edward about the Indians and their psychology, but when in 1938 she would go to India, her viewpoint was that of an honored guest at Government House.

Shortly after the Great War started, Edward was brought home and assigned responsibility for all overseas work in England, with special concern for the Indian troops, and was, therefore, on the spot when the United States entered the war in 1917. Imaginative, farsighted, and determined, he had to deal with a YMCA headquarters as blind and unprepared as was the U.S. government. He accomplished an heroic task, beset by criticism and incompetence, but he shaped it in his own spirit and was commended by General Pershing and the French government and awarded the Legion of Honor. Understanding and competent, Alice was party to all these activities.

To the great satisfaction of his sisters-in-law, Edward brought his family (now including three sons and a daughter) back to New York in 1922. There, for the next ten years, he worked for the general development of the skills of the conference table as preferable to the hazards of confrontation.

Alice was notably successful as a policy maker and active director on many boards, where her experience in the diverse activities of Edward's career surely reinforced her own natural abilities. She would become president, for a time, of each of the boards on which she served.

The Drapers after World War I

Charles Dana Draper was the most social of the Drapers, the most gracious, the most correct, the perfect gentleman of his period. With deep brown eyes and pink cheeks, he presented a conservative, immaculately fashionable appearance. He wore the correct clothes, spoke the proper language, played excellent tennis, sailed in the best boats, knew all the "right" people, and belonged to the best clubs.

He would spend his life on Wall Street, starting with the United States Trust Company. He then became a founding partner of McGraw, Blagden and Draper, Stock Brokers. He was totally dependable. He was always called "Charles."

He bought a narrow brownstone house at 174 East 72nd Street, where he entertained his friends—he had a great many friends—in a delightfully traditional manner. He had enormous charm. A younger relative said, "I always thought Charles was the apple of everyone's eye." He was wise and considerate and conventional, and a little remote. He was not a man of imagination, but he listened and understood. His was an absolutely lovely character.

At Cutler School and Harvard, Charles had been a track star, a half-miler. Always he was kind and encouraging to the younger lads on the team. Actively associated with the Madison Square Boys Club, he became president of its summer camp at Carmel, New York. This would be a lifelong concern. In the First World War, he was a naval officer and, as navigator in troop ships, made many Atlantic crossings.

Dorothea Draper was all character. Not tall, but compact and strong with concentrated force, she devoted herself to getting things done for the benefit of others; she exerted real influence. Inspired by the example of her sister Martha, and by nature a mover and shaker, Dorothea was one of the founding group of the Junior League. She had a good singing voice and was a leader in establishing the Schola Cantorum—a choral group of considerable prestige. She spent a large part of her great energies to further the Bellevue Hospital School of Nursing, the oldest such school in the United States. She had a fine, quirky sense of humor, but it was not always equal to the pressure of her concern that things be done in accordance with her own high standards.

Linzee Blagden, her husband, a conservative, nice man, was a vice president of The New York Trust Company. He worked for the education of the blind and for the New York Nursery and Children's Hospital. He and Dorothea had no children.

Ruth and Dorothea always addressed each other as "Davil," for they had some Irish thing going between them since childhood; Ruth's letters to Dorothea often went on in an exaggeratedly spelled-out brogue. As a child, Ruth turned to Dorothea for understanding, for comfort, and for advice. Even as she started on her first cross-country tour in 1915, she wrote back: "Davil mine—I depend on your wisdom and insight and strength. I will be very careful of myself." It took Ruth a long time to outgrow this dependence. Always she would admire Dorothea and look to her for stability.

"Cousin *George*—" said a much younger relative, her face brightening with remembered delight, "Cousin George was a wag! And a *little* bit naughty!"

Ruth said, "It is such a comfort to have him in the house with his gentle good cheer, lamb that he is, and being a doctor too." George, then, in 1906, was taking up his medical internship at the Presbyterian Hospital.

George was clever with his hands, clever with his mind—and had a clever wit and humor. He grew to be the tallest of the family, although as a skinny little kid, he had a sense of inferiority—others were so much taller and stronger and more favored than he. It was Charles, one year older, who first received a two-wheeled bicycle at Christmas. Hours later George was finally discovered in the cellar, trying to take a wheel off his three-wheeler, desperate because it didn't work. He grew to be good looking, though not so handsome as Charles, at whom he poked fun as the fashion plate, the socially correct man-about-town. But George greatly admired Charles for these qualities and was himself dapper and stylish, and very social.

There is a story told in the family that epitomizes the brothers. As they were strolling in the Park one Sunday morning, top-hatted and frock-coated, they were overtaken by a lovely lady on a runaway horse. Charles stepped neatly out of the way, but George flung himself at the horse's head, missed, and fell flat. The end of the ride is not recorded.

In his youth George was very social and remained a very good dancer whom the ladies loved for his gentle goodness, his humor and quality of fun—and for showing off to perfection his partners on the dance floor. But George was more than that. He was a sensitive man, imaginative, curious, and original. By nature a seeker, he could accept no assumption as the final answer but would search for more— more insight, more knowledge, more grasp of the whole man, the effect of mind on body. After four years of research in Germany, then at the Rockefeller Institute and the Pennsylvania Hospital studying the relationship of personality to the susceptibility of the patient to heart disease, infantile paralysis, and scarlet fever, he entered private practice, in 1912, and became an associate professor of clinical medicine at the College of Physicians and Surgeons. In World War I, as a lieutenant colonel in the U.S. Army Medical Corps, he was a consultant and epidemiologist.

In his book *Go East Young Man*, William O. Douglas, who became a Supreme Court judge in 1939, wrote an entire chapter on George Draper, whom he, as a young man, had consulted for migraine headaches and with whom he established a relationship almost of son to father.

In 1912 George had married Dorothy Tuckerman; their daughter Diana was born first, then George Tuckerman Draper in 1915, and Penelope somewhat later. Dorothy was a tall woman, large, impressive, and forceful; she urged George into an active Park Avenue social life—not congenial to a serious scientist. He was restless, frustrated, not really a happy person, and yet, with his great sensitivity, his delightful, playful humor, he gave much happiness to others. He never was dull.

Encouraged by her husband, Dorothy Draper became a well-known interior designer. She was notably successful in her dramatic decoration of large public spaces. They would divorce in 1931.

Martha Lincoln Draper, in addition to being a Draper, was also, on her mother's side, a Kinnicutt and a Waldo. Charles C. Burlingham, in a letter to *The New York Times* after her death, said: "Her perceptions were keen and immediate, her judgment was infallible. She knew when to speak and when to be silent. She was sympathetic and humorous. She knew how to grow old, for she had found wisdom and had understanding. And she was a great lady."

As Martha would live until 1943, the younger Drapers knew her well into their adult years. They called her "Barie" or "Ba," and she was part of their upbringing. For long periods, Ba would be in charge while Dr. and Mrs. Draper were in Europe. The Danas were nearby, and Aunt Fanny Macdaniel, but Ba was the one immediately on the job. Fourteen years younger than her stepmother and nineteen years older than Dorothea, Ba had it both ways. Embraced by the Danas as a favored daughter, they took her with them on their travels during the 1880s and 1890s to Europe and Egypt and the Holy Land.

In April 1887, when Mrs. Draper was thirty-seven and Paul, her sixth child, only four months old, she had a real breakdown, "exhausted [her] powers" she called it, and sailed to England for a change and rest. Will was there, and Aunt Ella, and they thought she might just be homesick—but she collapsed completely. Her husband was sent for and came immediately—in eight days of anxiety across the Atlantic. From Malvern she wrote to her "beloved daughter" Martha:

> I am slowly getting better—at least, I suppose I am. I am still very sad and cry easily and have a shrinking from getting back to my household and all of you if I am still to be as incapable as I felt myself. . . . I pray, and sometimes hope, that all the Brandy, Sal Volatile, arsenic and nux vomica, diversion, freedom from care and change of scene will pull me together again. I asked your father if he thought all this botheration taught him any wisdom by which he could help me from breaking up again, and he said "*no*."

Then she added: "If I die, I beg you not to use up your youth in the care of the children. Do what you can for your father but lead your own life. Do not give it up for the children." At some point, Mrs. Draper "gathered her powers," for her strength and force in the 1890s, until her death, have already been described. Her daughters, however, remembered "Mother's headaches" as frequent and lengthy.

In 1898, at the start of the Spanish American War, Martha joined the American Red Cross (ARC). When President McKinley granted permission for trained Red Cross nurses to minister to the wounded soldiers of the U.S. Army, Martha was sent to Charleston, South Carolina, in charge of twenty nurses. She remained there throughout the war. This was a historic breakthrough for women in wartime nursing in the U.S. Army.

When the United States entered the First World War, Martha rejoined the American Red Cross and, in July 1917, was sent abroad with Elizabeth Hoyt to study the activities and usefulness of women in the war zone, the requirements for refugee clothing, and the possible standardization of surgical dressings to be made by the ARC in the United States. In four months they completed a report that led to practical results. This is the same Elizabeth Hoyt with whom Ruth later dined in Paris in the company of General Pershing. After completing her assignment in the war zone, Martha, with the Red Cross rank of major, served for three years as assistant, and then director, of the ARC nonmedical personnel, enrolling and sending overseas nearly five thousand women.

Serious, intelligent, and forthright, Martha was gently spoken, quite mannish in dress and manner, but in no way masculine. She was "tweedy" and "smoked like a chimney," a gold clip of a cigarette holder almost constantly on her thin bony hand. Not at all pretty, Martha, in later years, had a pudgy full face and lips. She was small and strong. With Olivia Cutting, Martha purchased one of the first prefabricated portable houses and had it set up among the apple trees on a lovely piece of property in Lee, Massachusetts. They named it "Portapple," and Martha spent long summers there driving about the countryside in her Model A Ford. She ice-skated with the children, cut and tidied the tree stumps in the woods, tramped about in knickers, and helped to wash the dishes. She was an outdoor person who loved the land and the trees and the stars, so attuned to nature that she always said she thought she could feel the earth spinning.

In 1946, three years after the death of Martha, Ruth wrote Dorothea, whose husband, Harry James, had just undergone an operation for cancer:

> I'm glad Alice was around and was with you. I cried when I read your thought, and hers, of Ba—and what she would have been and done for you both. How blessed we are, to have had such a close and warm love binding us all—we four sisters—for so long, and that we turn to Ba still, as the surest and tenderest source of strength and the model of selflessness and behaviour (for want of a better word).

William Kinnicutt Draper, the eldest, was solid, an anchor. Closely resembling his father in appearance, he was a conventional man, a general practitioner in his father's footsteps, the traditional family doctor. With his pince-nez, his precise manner, and the big gold watch from Vienna, with its sweeping second hand, which Dr. Draper passed on to him in 1888, he must have taken pulses with comfortable reassurance.

Will had graduated from Columbia College in 1885 and from the College of Physicians and Surgeons in 1887. On the way to Dresden and Vienna for two years further study, he was briefly in London with Mrs. Draper who noted: "Will is very happy here. I think London suits him well with a new shiny hat and a flower in his buttonhole and his best coat on every day. He has just gone to lunch with Mrs. Phipps and to take little Paul [Phipps] to the great military tourney."

Will began private practice in New York in 1891, became professor of clinical medicine at the College of Physicians and Surgeons in 1910, and was on the staffs of both Bellevue and The New York Orthopedic Hospitals. The Children's Aid Society, where he was a trustee for fourteen years, recorded his accomplishment in bringing its medical work "to a state of high service . . . his presence was ever marked by a serene dignity and his work for the Society was inspired by ripe judgment and a keen sense of personal and professional responsibility."

In his beautiful script, with colored inks, Will wrote delightfully playful "puzzle letters" to his nephews. In 1898, Will married Helen Fidelia Hoffman, eldest daughter of Richard Hoffman, the well-known pianist who, as a very young man newly arrived in New York, became accompanist to Jenny Lind on her American concert tour in 1850. P. T. Barnum was their manager. Eight years younger than Will, then thirty-five, Helen was small, red-haired—"pink" she called it—delicate, often on the chaise-longue. A nephew remembers "her *beautiful* things." The presence of a cat threw her into hysteria. She and Will had no children.

Beginning with the Spanish American War in 1898, Helen devoted the energies of her lifetime to the American Red Cross. It filled her horizon and her conversation. Active in the New York State branch of the ARC, which she helped to form, she was appointed in 1917 chairman of the National Advisory Committee of Women of the War Council and later went abroad to assist in the demobilization of women ARC workers. She was instrumental in founding, through the Red Cross, the New York City health centers. She became a member of the boards of Bellevue Hospital, the Brearley School for Girls, the Florence Nightingale Foundation, and the Seeing Eye Foundation. Helen was decorated by France (Legion of Honor), Belgium, Serbia, and Germany for her war relief work.

Helen's much younger sister, Malvina, was a childhood playmate of Paul and Ruth Draper, who was the same age. After Will Draper's death in 1926, Helen would pursue her Red Cross activities and relief work in flood, drought, and depression, putting into effect her firm ideas of nutrition services. She suffered two strokes in 1948 and sadly lingered until January 1951, Ruth anxiously watching Malvina's endurance of this trial.

5

Onstage/Offstage

ÆOLIAN HALL, LONDON, JANUARY 29, 1920: Ruth Draper made her stage debut to a goodly house. Princess Beatrice, youngest daughter of Queen Victoria, was present, as well as royalty of the theatre—Ellen Terry, "laughing 'till she cried and had to wipe her eyes" and wearing, so it was reported, "one of her old-world hats, with flowing veil, three rows of bright red corals 'round her neck and enveloped in a black satin fur-edged cloak."

The die was cast, and only then did Ruth sail for home. Charles had his own apartment, and "Ba" had moved to Grove Street in Greenwich Village. Katherine Dreier's Societé Anonyme would hold its first exhibition of contemporary European paintings on the third floor of 19 East 47th Street, where Ruth had been born. A banner designed by Man Ray hung on the front of the house. Ruth had been away for sixteen months. A new era had begun.

This youngest sister who returned was not the youngest sister who had sailed off to war in 1918. She was confident, reserved about her own affairs, in control of her own life, earning her own way. The old family patterns had simply dissolved in the normal course of events, and Ruth now set about building her career in a world quite unknown to her brothers and sisters. As well as her position in the New York social world, she now, increasingly, would find a place in the social world of London.

From her youth, Ruth had been attracted to the richer, deeper culture of the European countries and, particularly, of England. In their civilized, urban worlds, she was as much at home as in New York—the different worlds to which she readily adapted and from which she drew nourishment.

Increasingly she sought the more fulfilling environment but never would feel herself in any sense an expatriate. From the perspective of the 1990s, how "modern" a woman she had become, independent and unafraid. In the first three years following her departure for the war zone in 1918, Ruth was to spend less than seven months in the United States. In the thirty-seven years following her debut in London, the years of her maturing talent and of her professional career, Ruth would be in the United States less than half of the time, and in a great part of these months at home, she would be on tour in the United States and Canada.

After only ten weeks at home, Ruth returned to England, sailing May 2, 1920, on the SS *Kronland* of the Red Star Line, for a tedious ten-day journey in a three-berth cabin with two other women.

Back in London, and comfortably settled in at 120 Ebury Street, she quickly established the pattern of her "cosy" mornings, the bed covered—as increasingly it would be—with letters, telegrams, newspapers, invitations, notes for monologues. This was where she wrote her letters, planned her days, thought about her monologues, telephoned her friends, and rarely got up before eleven.

On May 27 in Æolian Hall, *Ruth Draper* opened for a series of five weekly matinees, all sold out; she recited at an occasion at the Mansion House on June 22, twice at parties given by the "Dutchess [*sic*] of Norfolk," and she had engagements at forty-guinea fees ($210) nearly every day for three weeks. Then, at the insistence of her managers, she was booked at *the* Coliseum for two weeks beginning July 5 at a fee of one hundred pounds ($500) a week, which she thought very little. But to top the bill with "the adorable Grock," the supreme clown of his generation, was in itself a triumph—for she had, previously, given only six public performances in London.

Ruth was apprehensive, unexpectedly facing two weeks before a music hall audience—fearful of failure and lacking any experience of music halls. She was tired, and there was no time for rest, but she went on, trouper that she was rapidly becoming, and the extreme silence and great burst of applause told her that she could carry the vast space and a music hall audience of three thousand.

At some point Ruth must have written Ellen Terry of her pleasure in playing at the Coliseum, for there is an undated letter thanking Ruth for writing to tell her so and asking if she would be playing near London, as she "would like to go to see [her] again."

Friends came to her dressing room after the show; there were flowers and letters and telegrams. A new world had opened.

The reviews, without exception, were understanding of her work: "A dramatic artist, she is a hit of the season. As a mistress of gesture she is hard indeed to equal, versatile, rich, always vivacious, never vulgar." Her sketch, *The Actress*, was called "the most finished, delicate and brilliant. . . . A more highly individual art than hers is not to be conceived." The *Jewish Chronicle* reported on June 18:

> The art of Miss Draper stands alone. . . . To hold an audience enthralled for nearly two hours with this brand of dramatic art, without the aid of properties, music or scenery, is indeed a triumph. There is no doubt that her listeners would cheerfully have allowed Miss Draper to continue indefinitely.

And the *Westminster Gazette* on May 28 said:

> There is something almost uncanny in the insight and penetration distinguishing some of her delineation's, while not less remarkable is the

versatility which enables her to undertake the most widely contrasted impersonations with uniform success. She is altogether admirable.

Immediately following the Coliseum, Ruth had engagements of a week in Glasgow and in Manchester and Brighton, where she topped the bill twice nightly, for two weeks each. In October and November, she gave four additional performances at Æolian Hall in London. This completed her opening season. It was an extraordinary beginning.

"Dear Mrs. Phipps," Ruth reported to Dorothea, "is still a bit staggered by name in electric lights—but I don't feel that it changes me, my manners or morals in the least, it just amuses me."

With calm indifference, Ruth clearly was going against the norm of polite society. Women of respectable—and respected—families simply did not go on the stage. In England there was a long tradition of the theatre, going back hundreds of years, and Queen Victoria, under Albert's influence, was an avid theatergoer. While the war had changed many long-held judgments, people of the theatre—performing artists—were still held in questionable repute. Eyebrows were raised and heads shaken if a "lady" stepped over the footlights.

It was a triumph of her personal dignity and the sheer force of "self" that Ruth could, in 1928, be presented at Court by the wife of the American ambassador at the very time she was performing at the Haymarket Theatre, for this was a "social" presentation. Perhaps the fact that she simply "rose above" all negative implications gave Ruth considerable protection. She expected to be received, without qualification, at her normal social level. Her obvious quality of person, her dignity, the standard of deportment that she commanded were, of themselves, an armor. In her own theatre, hers was the sole influence; the stage was only where Ruth Draper worked, and she controlled its climate. She did not participate in events of theatrical life or style. Rarely, she would give a simple party in her own apartment—on her own "turf"—as for the cast of "The Chalk Garden." She appeared on stage at the Ellen Terry Memorial in Smallhythe (in 1955) and at the Eleanora Duse Memorial in 1929. In 1931 she rushed back to New York from her closing performance in Newark to lead the grand march with Ted Healy (then appearing in *The Gang's All Here!*) at the Stage Hand's Ball—the only such event recorded. Ruth did not mix her two worlds, the varied facets of her life would remain securely in place with no blurred edges. This was the unique position that she held throughout her professional career.

The 1920s were the years in which Ruth became firmly established on the European stage. Going from success in London to success in Paris, in Madrid, in Vienna, in Germany, and in Italy, one step led to another in what seemed almost to be a predetermined progression. Consistently she wrote, "Hundreds turned away—I could have stayed longer." Invariably she had not booked enough time; invariably she was astonished. She seemed never to quite believe it would happen.

These were the years in which her talent seemed to mature, her consciousness of technique develop, and her actor-audience relationships were nourished. The 1920s also were the years of Ruth Draper's greatest creative development. After 1929 she would present only one new sketch of substance, *Vive la France—1940*, a direct reaction to wartime emotions. These were the years in which Ruth finally accepted the validity of her talent and devoted herself to its perfection. Her Puritan need to know "God's will" must have been satisfied.

Muriel had stuck it out in London until May 1915, burning the last of the big studio church candles—because the electricity had been turned off weeks before—at a final night of music at Edith Grove, with Rubinstein, Ysaye, Barrere, Rubio and the London String Quartette, and, of course, Norman Douglas (who finally received the last bottles of Paul's really superb sherry). At dawn, all standing on the steps, to the strains of the Schubert Octet, they played her— with the two boys and Anxie, "the Irish angel" and nurse to the children—out of the house and into a taxi to her boat train. Edith Grove and its "musical euphoria" would be no more. Muriel had lost her gamble, too, for the war was not over by Christmas, not for three more years, and the only money forthcoming from home was for her return passage.

It has not been possible to establish the facts of Paul's life during the years since 1914, except that only the word *disaster* seems appropriate. For some months, we know from Ruth's letters, he was in the U.S. Army in charge of a unit of military police in France, thus raising Ruth's hope that the responsibility might steady him. But he seemed unable, for all his talent and charm, to grasp his life and to achieve a solid foothold. He and Muriel divorced, Ruth "lending" him the money. She told only Doro and Martha of this, for his brothers strongly disapproved. She also, secretly, "loaned" him money for his more pressing debts. She hoped she was right in taking the risk because she believed "that he seems more serious and determined and sincere to me and it may be the moment to help. . . . For the first time," she added, "I feel that our love, his and mine, means something real and helpful."

Then, in June 1920, Paul suddenly and impetuously married again. Muriel, very sportingly, gave him and "Peggy" a wedding breakfast at the Ritz. Ruth, stunned, wrote: "It's so queer that when I am on the top of the wave—like in 1914—the tragedy of his life should be like an undertow, but I am stronger now and there are other currents to test my resistance." Paul was trying for a stage job, but the play failed, and he began teaching. Ruth wrote: "[I am] determined not to let the worry and distress about Paul affect me as for many years it has. There is nothing to do but steel oneself to be prepared for the new troubles that are bound to come." As the situation had worsened over the years, Ruth had repeated what she had said at his marriage in 1909. "I can't bear to cut off." But now, at the urgent and insistent indignation of George, his family had closed all communication with Paul. This was, for Ruth, a time of deep trauma.

In 1941, from Chicago, she wrote to Martha of a day spent with old friends, Anne Richardson and her husband George, who was a "school-day friend of Paul's.

They were lovely to him in those sad days when he was in Chicago with Peggy and we had cut him off. The pain and remorse for that stupid decision still wrings my heart when I think of it. George and Anne loved Paul and admired Peggy. I often wonder what became of her. God grant I never do anything so cruel again in my life."

Early in 1924, she decided to remain at home to do what she could to give some stability to Paul's life. They gave joint recitals during the summer resort season, and in the fall she occupied the house of Mrs. Douglas Robinson, Corinne Alsop's mother, where she was able to have Paul with her and where he sang at the Christmas party that she gave there. Paul continued to give concerts and was to sing the *St. Matthew Passion* under Mengelberg, when, on February 15, while attending a large and festive party in the Gramercy Park home of Robert Chanler, he suddenly dropped dead. His many years of drug and alcohol abuse had finally taken their toll. In the general shock and consternation, it seemed imperative to avoid an investigation, which would have involved the other guests, who were in no way connected with this event. Acting quickly and impulsively, two of Paul's friends, placing his hat and overcoat on his lifeless body, "walked" him across the street to a room he had rented and laid him on the bed, where a maid found him the next morning. Thus, the dramatic, and macabre, end to his disastrous life.

In the published comments after Paul's death, it was the consensus that "with the slenderest of vocal equipment but with taste, instinct and musical intelligence he accomplished much." The funeral service was held two days later at Grace Church, where as a small boy he had sung in the choir. Young Paul, aged fifteen, sat in the pew behind his uncles and aunts, but Muriel, rebuffed by Ruth, sat at the back of the church. "Smudge" was in Woodstock and did not feel that he wanted to come down for the service; "he was so shy and withdrawn and such a little boy" at age eleven. Ruth wrote to Lucy Ann Whitaker: "Of course I understood and it was right to do what 'Smudgy' felt he wanted. In a way I am sorry he should not have seen the crowd of friends who paid tribute to all that was fine in his father."

Ruth so deeply loved this younger brother, the inseparable companion of her childhood; they were perfectly in tune with one another. With all his elegance and humor and charm, he yet, according to Alice, was "irresponsible and lacked the strong common sense and moral side of Ruth." Years later, writing to Alice, Ruth reminisced: "I can hear him laugh and see him walking over the grass with that wonderful free step. No one ever walked or laughed with such grace and gaiety."

Muriel often said, "Paul went off with Jeanne Eagels and never came back." Although the story has come down to the next generation of Drapers, the actual timing proves elusive, and it may be apocryphal. However, given Paul's temperament, it is certainly not impossible. It runs like this: Paul was booked to make his debut in a London concert, but, strolling down the street one afternoon, he encountered Jeanne Eagels, an old friend, who had been playing in Somerset Maugham's *Rain*, in which she had made her great success. Paul told her of his upcoming concert, and Jeanne Eagels is reputed to have replied, "No, you're not singing a concert, you're sailing back to New York tomorrow morning, with me." And so he did. At any rate, it is an entertaining black-sheep story that merits recording—with the caveat that although part of the family mythology, it stands unsupported.

There was no more Ruth could do for her adored Paul, but the anguish and regrets remained. She went off to work, and a trip to Greece, but the boys held her concern. Their mother remained in New York, as an interior decorator. The Drapers were wary of Muriel: her "Bohemian" way of life, her exotic appearance, her manner—Rubinstein describes her "brusque, self-assertive ways, sarcastic remarks and loud laughter, made of a completely different mettle." They blamed Muriel for inspiring Paul's gambling; however that may be, it is certain that he ran through all her money as well as his own. They were apprehensive about her influence with Paul's sons, but, after all, she was their mother, and, as Ruth said, "There isn't anything we can do about it." Ruth and Dorothea worried about young Paul and Smudge—with no money, no settled home, and their mother hardly a homebody. It was a problem they could never resolve.

Both boys suffered from the lack of a stable home and a mother on the job, but Paul enjoyed his unorthodox childhood and loved his colorful mother, an artist as he was. Smudge, possibly with less imagination, perhaps less of an artist, did not have so much fun. But both boys grew to manhood, apparently with not too many complexes, in spite of their aunts' anxieties. Muriel's granddaughter, Anne, remembers with happiness and gratitude the enchantment and excitement of a walk down Fifth Avenue with her grandmother, who built wonderful stories about the people they saw and fantasies about everything in the shop windows, stimulating the child's imagination and fully participating in the fun. In later years, with young Paul married to Heidi and with three small daughters, Muriel seemed to enjoy her role as grandmother, for she was "in and out of the house a great deal."

After visiting in Brussels, Ruth set off for a holiday to Vienna, Budapest, and—via Belgrade and Sofia—Constantinople, where she had her first taste of "Empire"—which in later tours to South Africa and to India she would thoroughly appreciate. She described it in a letter to Anxie:

> Turkey was very fascinating and strange and that queer flavor of the East that you don't really know until you go there. We can never really mix, or understand them. I nearly went crazy in the Bazaar! The 10 days in Constantinople were delightful—in many ways I feel I would have got more out of it had I not been quite so comfortably immersed in the British Empire! Really, the power of the British to carry themselves into strange places, and establish a bit of England wherever they go, is simply amazing. Such comfort, such order and regularity of life, such promptness and familiar details! Same hot water can, with a towel tucked around it, same food, same gloomy church service and long

parson, same intense interest in the weather, and unstylish clothes—it's a thick safe enveloping atmosphere—way off there in Turkey with mystery and history and tragedy and romance all around—but *they* are in England for the Union Jack flies over their heads!

Then on to an exhausting ten days of sightseeing in Greece: "A dream of beauty—such a different world one had to completely change one's point of view and one's emotional response. Often I was on the verge of tears just because of the beauty and the simplicity of the message of the great past that came through so clearly."

On October 25, on the way home, Ruth wrote to Lucy Ann Whitaker: "I'm better and have my old energy back, for I realize how precious a thing my work is and that I owe it all the courage and enthusiasm I can summon. Paul and my work were the two realities, the two anchors in my life; with him gone the other is doubly precious—particularly as he loved it so and was so ambitious for me. It's terribly hard coming home for the first time without him being there and I seem to miss him more rather than less as time goes on."

Back in New York, Ruth went straight off on tour and was in Boston the first week in December, where Lady Diana Cooper saw her in "a crowded dark little drawing room full of Boston ladies watching a German adventurer calling himself Baron something . . . who did the most shocking dances of the Macabre school semi-naked, in a Picasso-designed dress, with his naked parts covered in blood and smelt the place out with amber scent. . . . Ruth Draper was there," Diana reported to Duff, "quite disgusted and terribly grand—with no hope of a stunt in her."

During these years, Ruth was establishing her own quiet style in dress—clean lines, good materials, careful colors, clothes one could move in, for she was very active. As time went on she bought from the best houses, dressmakers, and tailors. Her shoes were custom made in England and Italy, well-fitting shoes—she walked a great deal. Except for summer tennis and swimming and her boats, walking was the exercise she depended on to stay healthy—ever an all-important consideration. She wore beautifully cut English tweed suits. Particularly remembered was a reddish-brown tweed that she sometimes wore when walking in the park with a friend—a neighbor's Irish setter, whose coat exactly matched her suit. Other walkers turned to watch, for woman and dog, full of vitality and pleasure in each other's company, were so obviously enjoying a brisk autumn morning.

A good "home cook" herself, Ruth loved good plain food, fresh and lots of it. Joyce Grenfell wrote, "Ruth spooned in very fast and was ready for seconds before anyone else." Crème fraîche, fraises des bois, crème brûlee—these were treats to be savored. Much as she loved England, she thought wistfully of the early lima beans she might be having at home. In Paris she happily indulged in fine French food, gaining pounds, as she did in Maine with thick fresh cream on her morning porridge, and then spent the winter taking it off.

Ruth made many visits to Fontainebleau to stay with the Walter Gays. There she could take long walks in the "forét" and "let her voice out" in the tirade of *The Actress* and other "full voice" characters. She talked to herself a great deal— in her stage characters or a momentary character, just passing by. At Islesboro or near a lake, abroad, she might row out, singing and talking to herself—there seemed to be another life going on in her mind. At heart she was a solitary, but as time went on and the complexity of her life increased she had less and less time to be solitary without other lives impinging upon hers. Her mornings in bed provided the opportunity, but as letters from her "fans" multiplied, this time to herself was given over to responding, for no letter went unacknowledged, a point of courtesy upon which she prided herself.

Ruth Draper's intense concentration, the convinced projection of her charac- ters, audibly reached a level of audience conviction in *The German Governess*, who entered—eyes watering and nose running—saying through her sniffles, "*Guten morgen*, children. Now say, 'Good morning Fraulein.'" Some in the audience re- sponded, "Good morning, Fraulein," quite seriously participating as her students.

With a responsive, alert audience sharing the fun—for fun she considered it to be—her "character" bloomed, new lines being spoken and sometimes an en- tirely new incident being played out, often running a sketch two, three, even four minutes beyond its usual time. Ruth always held that this was not her doing; the character was in control and reacting normally. There was nothing she, Ruth Draper, could do about it; she merely embodied the individual onstage.

Her stage manager, Charles Bowden, was concerned about time—the audi- ence might grow tired. But Ruth said, "Oh, I always feel that before they do and then I stop." Spontaneity—dealing with stage problems as they arose—was the key to her work. No wonder the cop on the beat came in to listen to the language and accent whenever she played the old Irish woman—"It could be my own mother!"—or the stage hands gave up their usual crap game to gather in the wing, watching her—"My *greatest* compliment," she said.

The simple fact that she was performing on a stage, in a theatre, seemed to add strength to Ruth's performances. Working on a platform somehow lowered her sense of "theatre," of professionalism. Platforms were more usual in captive- audience or subscription situations. But when onstage, Ruth knew that her audi- ence had paid, of their own choice, to hear her—psychologically so very different.

Some of her audiences were a real trial. In Boston, paying for their seats, one full house responded not at all—not a laugh, not a clap—absolutely dead. When she came off, having cut her sketches as much as was reasonable, her nephew Paul asked her how she felt, working against this blank wall. "It was like sawing wood, wasn't it?" she said.

Paul felt that Aunt Ruth "did not really know the rigors of the theatre," even though her letters report a considerable range of audience reactions. However, she went through her entire career with little knowledge of lighting or stage-manage- ment techniques in her own work.

As she told Charles Bowden, when he took over as her stage manager at the

Empire Theatre in New York in 1947: "Script? What script? Cues? Don't make it so complicated. You ring up the curtain, I go on; when I'm finished I come off and you ring down the curtain. It is perfectly simple." When Bowden spoke of union rules and overtime, she dismissed the problem: "Oh, the Union has always been very kind to me."

Ruth Draper's financial arrangements were, possibly, unique. She waved aside talk of "investors." "I don't want anyone to gamble on me." And of costs and guarantees, she said: "I give you a check for the cost of mounting the show and two weeks into the run you pay me back. After that we divide the profits equitably. You can't guarantee this? You don't have to guarantee it, you can just give it to me." Which is exactly what happened over the next ten years with Charles Bowden.

Ruth was more than a little in awe of theatre people; she never entered into the theatrical social life. And of all theatre people, she was closest to her English dressers—simple, uncomplicated, and devoted in their care and support of her over many years—notably "my beloved Ada, she just suits me."

Time and again Ruth was asked to give interviews. Time and again she said, as in a letter to Mrs. William Brown Meloney of *The New York Herald Tribune:* "I suppose I am very stupid to refuse, and that I seem ungrateful, but I prefer to continue to give my impressions through my work." Nor would she write about her work or about herself: "I hate interviews and confessions. The article you may have seen was not of my doing!" Her public image remained securely *behind* the footlights.

Ruth was now firmly established as a presence in society and a figure of professional prestige, dignity, and competence. From Ellen Terry down, the "theatre greats" flocked to see her perform, to learn what they could from a talent inherent and impossible to communicate. They were in awe of her.

Ruth's strength and force and power onstage, so unexpected by Elisabeth Draper (newly wed to George), left Elisabeth stunned and incredulous, "completely overcome." Nothing had prepared her for the difference: Ruth "in life"—the quiet, humble, self-effacing youngest sister—and the onstage presence of assurance and potent command. Forty years later, in speaking of the shock, Elisabeth could only say, "I have never got over it—it was extraordinary."

Katharine Hepburn summed it up: "My God, how brilliant she was!—with her essential, her enormous personal distinction. What fascinated me was to see this *enormously* distinguished creature turn into a peasant—*instantly!*"

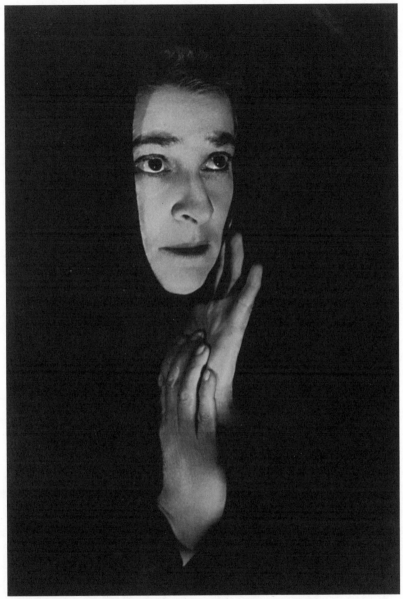

Vive la France—1940, London, 1946. Photo by Angus McBean.

Ruth Draper with Theater in der Josefstadt poster, Vienna, June 1956. Photo by Trude Fleichmann.

Charcoal drawing of Ruth Draper by John Singer Sargent before seeing her perform, London, 1913

Eunice Dana Brannan (Aunt Nin), Ruth holding baby Diana, and Mrs. Draper, Mt. Kisco, July 1914

Ruth Draper at a costume ball, Paris, 1922

Lauro de Bosis, Portonovo, 1920. Photo by Charis de Bosis. (By permission of Arturo Vivante and the Houghton Library, Harvard University, bMS ital 65 [13])

Lauro de Bosis *(left)* with his sister Elena Vivante, Leone Vivante, and their first child, Paolo, Rome, October 1921. (Courtesy of Paolo Vivante)

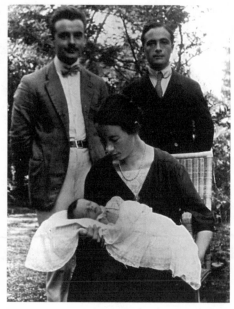

Living room of Ruth Draper's apartment at 66 East 79th Street, New York, c. 1938.
Photo by Drix-Duryea.

Ruth Draper at Islesboro with Salvemini and Anne Draper reading *The Wind in the Willows*, c. 1943. Photo by Roberto Bolaffio.

Ruth Draper at Islesboro with seven small English visitors and two friends, c. 1943

Ruth Draper sails her twelve-foot boat, the *Flickamaroo*

Raimund Sanders Draper ("Smudge"), RAF, England, c. 1942

Ruth Draper and her nephew Paul Draper, Edinburgh, 1951.
Photo by Edward Drummond Young.

Ruth Draper, c. 1950. Photo by Dorothy Wilding.

Ruth Draper onstage in *Opening a Bazaar.* Photo by Muray

Ruth Draper offstage *(right)* opens *The Mudlark*, with Gretchen Green, for charity, Thames Barge at Windsor, June 11, 1951. Photo by *The Windsor Express*.

Ruth Draper as the Grandmother in *Three Generations in a Court of Domestic Relations*. Photo by Trude Fleischmann.

Ruth Draper as Mrs. Clifford in *Three Women and Mr. Clifford*, New York, c. 1950. Photo by Trude Fleischmann.

Ruth Draper, London, 1951. Photo by Angus McBean.

Ruth Draper listens to playback of RCA recording, New York, 1954. (Courtesy of RCA)

Ruth Draper laughs at playback of RCA recording, New York, 1954. (Courtesy of RCA)

Ruth Draper, Vienna, June 1956

Ruth Draper, New York, December 11, 1956

6

Glory and Grief

DURING ALL OF RUTH'S YOUNG YEARS—and her young years stretched nearly to thirty-four—dominated by her mother, she was shy, not assertive, not a vital person. If there were flickers of romance, they were not noted in any letters that have survived. Her sisters Alice and Dorothea said they never knew the concerns of her heart, for "she kept everything to herself." After Harriet Marple and Aileen Tone grew into friendship of unreserved confidentiality, it is in letters to them that one finds mention of her longings, her sparks of hope, and their dimming.

Most serious, during her performances for the American troops in 1919, was Ruth's attraction to a handsome, very charming American officer from North Carolina, six years her junior. They rode together, her eyes sparkled, but already, she found, he was engaged. His fiancée died, and again Ruth hoped. They met occasionally in New York as he passed through Pennsylvania Station; there was a carriage drive in Central Park. Then, finally and clearly, she knew this was not to be, for he had married someone else. Ruth wept easily, but now she wept long, often, and deeply—heavy, wracking sobs. "No one," said Mildred Graves at Chapel Hill, "no one ever sobbed so uncontrollably." Yet it was the dream she had lost—only the dream—not the reality.

This happened again and again—though not to the same degree—until one wonders how much the romantic vision was hers alone. How often, she told Harriet Marple years later, there seemed to be a spark—and she thought, this time, perhaps—but then the eyes glazed and the spark died. Perhaps, too, there came a point in the relationship when her New England reserve, the innocence of the Victorian woman, perhaps her eagerness, became a barrier, and her unreadiness to make the inevitable concessions became apparent. Then, too, Ruth's fame was steadily increasing; she had become a somewhat public figure—*in* the theatre but not of the theatre world—*of*, in fact, an enviable and well-connected social world. Her pattern of life was becoming established. It must have been apparent to any man of experience that her "work" was a compulsion not to be denied. Ruth had much attention, many beaux, and one or two suitors stood waiting many years to "serve and comfort" her. But basically she could not bring herself to limit her freedom.

She recognized her "constitutional balking at making any binding commitment." This carried down to even so minor a commitment as to say when she would reach London for a well-publicized season. She preferred to arrive, go to a hotel, or her rented house, settle in, and then, *then* to ring up, saying brightly: "It's Ruth! I'm *here!*" She was sorry, sometimes, for there had been a dinner party, or a special concert, and "had they only known." But she never changed; her freedom of action was more important.

"Hold me close in your heart and pray for me," she wrote to Aileen Tone from St. Moritz, "that I may have more courage, more light and more strength to endure pain—such as I've not felt before. I can't write more—say nothing to a soul—because there is nothing to say. I am well—I am always with friends. I see my way plainly—work, distractions of travel and new experiences, and faith in the purpose and end of renunciation. It must be to serve some vague plan. Again must I try and use suffering to make beauty and laughter. Again!"

In Berlin, early in 1928, Max Reinhardt presented Ruth Draper in six performances, then to Vienna, in Reinhardt's Theater an der Josefstadt, for two performances. She wrote Harriet: "The most beautiful theatre I've ever seen—I've had perhaps the triumph of my life. . . . They say no one had anything to equal it—not even Duse and [Yvette] Guilbert. They thought me quite mad to leave such a success. However, I've seen several eyes glow and hearts flutter, but none have had a like effect on me." Back, then, to Munich and Frankfort for one performance in each, on to Florence for a ten-day visit and five sold-out performances at the Teatro dei Fidente. On March 1 she arrived in Rome, exhilarated and exhausted, nervously, physically, emotionally drained.

Settled in at the Hotel de la Ville, on the via Sistina, every day she saw friends, attended parties—there were many who wished to meet her—she gave four performances at the Teatro Quirinetta, as well as a few private recitals. On the 14th, in the afternoon, and on the initiative of the American ambassador, her friend William Garrett, she performed for Mussolini at the Palazzo Venezia. As she walked down the long, vast room toward him she was greeted courteously, although he appeared nervous—shortly before this an English woman had made an attempt on his life. When the Duce's invited guests had assembled, a maid entered carrying Ruth Draper's shawls, rolled up, under her arm. Several years later, Ruth recounted to Neville Rogers this experience of the Duce's agitation:

> Then I saw for a moment what lay behind that facade of grandeur and bellicose power. The great ruler seemed suddenly petrified. He flung up his arms in front of his face. "Via! Via!" he cried ("Take it away!"). As the maid spread out the shawls and the expected explosion did not occur, his efforts to recover his dignity were so pathetic that I couldn't help feeling sorry for the poor little man. Fortunately I had a brain wave. I pulled my handbag partially open and contrived to drop it. Its contents flew all over the floor, and everybody bent down to retrieve them. As the Duce handed me my lipstick, there was a big burst of laughter from the assembled *gerarchi* [Hierarchs—

the accepted name in Italy for the Fascist bigwigs], and nobody laughed louder than he did.

The next day, her diary records: "Flowers from Mussolini."

At a luncheon that same day in the Palazzo Borghese apartment of her friend the Marchesa Presbitero—an American and a painter—Ruth met Lauro de Bosis, handsome, dynamic, half American, wholly Italian, of unbelievable charm, a poet, and aged twenty-six. Ruth was vital, beautiful, a mature actress widely acclaimed throughout Europe, yet with a youthful purity of spirit that de Bosis must rarely have encountered in his own sophisticated Roman world. Three days later they met in the evening at Contessa Pasolini's, and on the 19th he drove her to Frascati, to dine at Alfredo's and to see a Pirandello play. Then, for the next twenty days, they met for some part of each day. On the 21st and 22nd, he attended two of her three performances at the Teatro Odescalchi, watching ecstatically "this miracle," for until then he had not seen her in performance.

Against her diary entries for March 23, 24, and 25, she wrote, "Divino amore!" On the 27th, they both lunched with the Marchesa Presbitero, then walked and talked all afternoon under the trees on the Palatine. After tea with Nina de Cesaro, Lauro took Ruth to meet his mother—she recited—and two evenings later dined with Signora de Bosis in her apartment at 66, via Due Macelli, at the Piazza di Spagna, and had coffee on the terrace overlooking Rome to the west.

Ruth and Lauro's mother were of similar English stock and pioneering New England background and met without reservation. Signora de Bosis was tall and straight, with grace and distinction, wearing always the long gray, or mauve, or black dresses, the rustling dresses, of her young womanhood in Italy—dresses of beautiful material with fine laces. At the age of six, she had come to Italy, where her father, the Reverend Doctor Le Roy Vernon, would establish the first Methodist Episcopal Church in Italy. Lillian had been about twenty-three when she met Adolfo de Bosis; he was vibrant, handsome, rather dapper, and with great charm. Both were in thrall to Percy Bysshe Shelley, whose poems Adolfo would translate into Italian, as well as those of Walt Whitman and the classical Greek poets. Adolfo and Lillian were married in 1890. Lauro was the youngest of their eight children; all were diverse in interests and talent, good looking and with the family's cultivation and charm. Adolfo de Bosis, who had died in 1924, was himself an unusually cultured and delightful intellectual, a friend of the most interesting and important men of his time—writers, musicians, artists, and thinkers. He was a lawyer and businessman, but primarily a man of letters. He was attorney and counsel to Eleanora Duse, who was a constant presence in the family. D'Annunzio, that flamboyant political and literary figure, Fascist sympathizer, womanizer, and boyhood friend of Adolfo's, came and went—but his influence lingered. Shelley was the household God. Everything in Lauro's background was, for Ruth, not only reassuring but attractive. She was, in fact, enchanted.

Lauro de Bosis lost no time in declaring his admiration and romantic interest, expressed always in the most extravagantly poetical of terms drawn from his great familiarity with literature and mythology. For Lauro, to feel an emotion was to express it—instantly and without deliberation or consideration. Ruth was overwhelmed; though captivated, she was confused and more than a little frightened, for his approach was of a directness, of a passion and insistence for which she was in no way prepared. Her experience, leaving aside Arthur Rubinstein and the international group of musicians of her brother Paul's Edith Grove days, had really been limited to American and British men—to gentlemen of her own social circle whose code of courtesy and behavior—which she took for granted—held gentle respect for this brilliantly talented but ingenuous American woman. Clearly she was attracted to Lauro de Bosis—so extravagantly romantic an Italian man—but she had not the slightest idea of how to deal with him. She longed for the love he offered, but it was too much, too strong, too soon. She spoke with Katherine Presbitero of the great doubts torturing her, of her distress and dismay at the turn of events, of her reluctance to leave Rome—perhaps never to see Lauro again; yet every instinct told her to adhere to her schedule, to give herself time to think, unassailed by this whirlwind of emotion. On Saturday, April 7, Ruth and Lauro talked for hours, walking together in the Gardens of the Villa Medici. Then he took her to the six o'clock train to Florence.

A few days later Lauro called on Katherine Presbitero, miserable that he had brought pain to Ruth, wracked by doubts, but happy and proud. She wrote to Ruth, "My dear, *his charm*! I have rarely seen anything like it!"

As none of Ruth's letters to Lauro appear to have survived (undoubtedly she destroyed them), one must look to Lauro's letters for an indication of her state of mind.

Lauro's first letter, written April 9, begins, in his awkward English:

My beloved archangel—

since I saw you disappear at the station I have felt like a madman and a criminal for having let you go away from me and not sooner enchained you. . . . I have passed dreadful hours. . . . Now I am much more serene and feel that I see again clearly enough the "wisdom" of the terrible decision we have taken. I feel proud of the conquest over ourselves. . . . Through you, I too, have drunk the milk of Paradise and will never more be the same as before. My soul is full of blessing and vague prayers and I feel almost the need of kneeling down. Thank you! Thank you! I feel on my spirit the seal of yours. And I look to the future, to our future too, with faith and love. I kiss your hands with worship and adoration.

It was signed "Lauro de Ruth."

There was in him an elusive, intriguing quality of real romanticism, of the innate poet, that was given free rein in his approach to a woman, even in the most casual of social encounters. There are other letters, to other women, in earlier years, that are signed "Lauro de Nancy," "Lauro de X," and, probably, "Lauro de Y" and "de Z." There are other letters that contain, word for word, the same extravagant phrases in describing his love. Florid romanticism, well schooled by the poets, was his natural language, which had, each time, the quality of a fresh revelation; he was, himself, captivated by his own words. But now, *this* love, so sudden, so intense, of such star quality, was no light-hearted fancy. After the first letters to Ruth, there is a new tone, a deeper chord. In Ruth, he had found another romantic, responsive yet reluctant, perhaps unattainable. He was no less confused than she. Neither really understood the other, yet each was enchanted with the image they saw. Her purity and innocence were a new and unexpected factor.

He now proposed a plan: He could borrow a villa on the Adriatic, near Ancona. Would she come there? They could see interesting and lovely places, sail and swim and "take a suitcase of wonderful books of poetry." He would ask his friend Giorgio de Santillana and his wife to stay there, too; "they would hardly be seen except at meals and they would create an atmosphere that would allow you to come without any hesitation or moral problem because coming would not involve anything. Then if love came to you, unaware, the mountain top would become not only a platonic cenacle but a love nest. . . . But perhaps I made a big mistake hinting that entire love might come. *You must not think at all* about such a possibility or else the old problem comes up again and we must escape problems. Write to me immediately. I am burning."

A few days later, to her response, he wrote: "I am awfully sorry if something in my letter (I hardly remember what I wrote) made you believe that I *really* regretted not to have lured you and forced you more." But his real regret was that he did not control himself more "because probably if I had let you see only my friendship and veneration we might have gone on peacefully for 2 months." Two days later: "Letters are such terrible traps: I see that mine gave just the contrary impression to the one I meant to convey. I don't love anything any more that is not in some way connected with you. . . . What a miracle to have such a touchstone." He came to Florence, to a different hotel, for three days. They toured the nearby towns and had tea with Berenson, who at once saw the state of affairs. Ruth wrote a two-page list, day by day, of all their meetings; it is headed "Lauro—here is the record of our happy days."

And again he wrote: "What a royal and devine [*sic*] thing it is to be Ruth Draper's Knight! To wear her colours, to feel somehow her eyes looking on you, to hold as one great goal to become more worthy of those eyes, to judge all things from their standard! I feel as if I were the only man in the world to have the golden spurs! . . . Have you peace at last, my beloved? Could I not do anything to change your tormented eyes, when you so much did for mine? Won't you try to love more yourself for my sake?" Almost daily there was page after page in the same vein and on May 1st he concluded: "If I had to choose between the power of making you love *me* or of making you love your great art, I think I would choose the second! Ah! Your unborn sketches! I am craving toward them!"

Romantic, indeed, these letters, but hardly the letters of a grown man to a mature woman of forty-three. Ruth, however, was not a mature woman; emotionally she was an adolescent, starry-eyed and totally inexperienced. Suddenly she had the love she had longed for, but it was of an immediacy, an intensity beyond her ability to adjust. From the ship en route home she wrote to Harriet, "Never have I dreamed that such love and such beauty could come to me." She was baffled, terrified, and, as so often before, overcome by her sense of unworthiness, her "suffering."

Ruth went directly to Dark Harbor, her emotions crowded by concern for all the family children for whom she had planned this special summer. "They should know me before I begin to break up!" Later in July Lauro wrote: "You wonder, in your last letter, whether it would be better for us to keep the image of these days we had above the danger of being spoiled or diluted by anything else. You say you have great powers to hurt me by disappointing me. . . . Whether it will be better for your peace that I should not come to America I will probably understand it through the lines of your letters next Fall; if I do I will be capable of renouncing to it without bitterness. I will be waiting for 'presages.'" Late in August she received another letter. He was in a quandary. Would his presence be a disturbance? The serenity of her letters made him think this was so and that perhaps he should wait. "You don't really want me to come, do you? Or at least you are more afraid of it than desirous." He reiterated his adoration and that he remained stretching his hands and soul to her across the sea, but at one word: "I'll run to you. Run as to myself, because only near you, in you, I have felt that I was something, that I was living and have only to turn to you to find a reason, a light, a faith in everything." Again he signs, "Lauro de Ruth."

Dated August 26, 1928, Lauro sent her a poem:

A R. D.

In questa chiara notte siderale
la Terra si congiunge con il cielo
e traluce oltre il mistico suo velo
l'anima de le cose universale.

L'anima mia dilegue come un frele
fior che si sfogli da un aereo stelo
al caldo vento ch'esso bevve, anelo
ed ebbro per la morte che l'assale.

Poi che in tale notte ti seguii
librato nel tuo spirito canoro,
oltre le stelle nel supremo coro,

il tuo solo pensiero mi conduce
di là dai mondi a immergermi nei pii
fonti da cui si genera le luce.

To R. D.

In this clear starry night
the earth joins the sky
and the universal soul of things
shines through its mystic veil.

My soul fades like a frail flower
on its aerial stem, its leaves
plucked by the warm wind it drank, inebriated
and longing for the death that assails it.

Since on such a night I followed you
borne aloft by your melodious spirit,
in the supreme choir beyond the stars,

your thought alone leads me
beyond the worlds to immerse myself
in the sacred fonts from which light is born.

(Translation by Arturo Vivante)

Reassured that the Italy-America Society would not be a conduit for Fascist propaganda, Lauro accepted the position of executive secretary—he needed a job and *there* was Ruth. But he remained wary of Fascist influence.

From Dark Harbor, Ruth arrived by bus in Avon, Connecticut, to visit Corinne Alsop. From there, on the 11th, she wrote to Harriet:

> I've gotten to the point of "near" terror at the thought of the meet-ing—and woke at four this morning sure that I hated the idea of seeing him and had no love for him at all. I certainly was not made for love affairs and it's well I've had so few of this variety. I can hear you roaring but this particular joke can go no further just now!
>
> Everything of course is perfectly indefinite until I hear from Lauro. . . . Corinne proposes he come here—we shall be alone and it's so lovely and quiet and she is going to be away until Sunday night. I've written him to propose this—hope he will phone on his arrival.

That was Thursday. Lauro arrived. He went to Avon, and together they returned to New York on Sunday. Ruth took a room at the Westbury Hotel on Madison Avenue at 69th Street for six weeks while her new apartment was being painted and made ready for her occupancy.

Lauro renewed his ardent pursuit and saw Ruth constantly. His approach was determined, practiced, clearly that of a lover. There was no word of marriage. It was not long before love triumphed. Lauro was euphoric. He wrote to her on tour: "I know for sure, that it is going to be all right also for you in every sense and I tremble with emotion, thinking that it is I that the Gods have chosen to bring you love."

Ruth held the illusion that people "didn't know!" Alice said, "I wonder why she bothers, we *all* know!" One had only to see them together—"like two children," said Laura White, embarrassed, "Ruth behaved like an infatuated schoolgirl." Corinne Alsop knew, thought the affair unwise, did not at all approve, but, as an old and close friend, thought she should be supportive. She took Ruth to her own doctor for a sex talk.

This was a difficult time for Ruth's family and friends. Even in 1975, the son of one of her friends said, with a shrug of his shoulders, "Well, after all, she was *on the stage*." But George approved, for he thought Ruth "gun-shy." Laura White, her childhood friend, thought "gun-shy," too. She did not like Lauro, though she never said why—it was an intuitive feeling, for she had grown up in a sophisticated Roman society.

This was Ruth's first, her greatest, and, probably, her only real love affair. Years before, she had asked Mildred Graves: "When two people wish to go away together, where do they go? How do they do it?" And she added, "I'll be lonely—I *am* lonely, but I could never live with a woman." Many years later, her nephew, Paul, who should have known better, asked her if she had had other affairs. Ruth made no response.

Ruth's career pursued its course. On Christmas night she opened at the Comedy Theatre in New York and, with crowded houses, ran eight performances a week to April 29 (1929)—nearly eighteen weeks. On May 18 she sailed, with Lauro, for a few days in Paris. He returned to Rome, and she left for Warsaw to perform—with Arthur Rubinstein, Syzmanowski, the Kochanskis, and the Mylnarskis as her escorts in Poland. After a five-day trip to Moscow and St. Petersburg—shattered by the conditions she found there—she fled to Vienna and Venice, where Lauro met her for six days. They flew to Ancona and went on to the Torre di Portonovo, a very old watchtower that was the summer home of the de Bosis family. Reached by a steep path down the hillside, it stood so close to the Adriatic Sea that at high tide it seemed to rise from the water. "A wild and most beautiful spot."

Signora de Bosis was there, two sisters with three little nephews, and Lauro's brother, Vittorio, a doctor in Florence. From way along the beach, Ruth wrote to Ba. She had stripped for a swim and sat drying off "in a state of nature." There was only sky and sea; far out the black-hulled fishing boats with their colored sails were working their way across the water. She was deeply happy.

Ruth established an immediate rapport with Lauro's mother, who noted that with the simplicity and understanding of a true artist, Ruth adapted to their easygoing camp life. The tower was austere; the bedrooms small, sparely furnished as a monk's cell, with an iron bed and an armoire; the dining room with a big wooden table and rustic chairs with woven rush seats and buffet shelves on the wall, as in so many Italian country houses. Actually, Ruth loved it; the easy simplicity just suited her. As effortlessly as she slipped into their family life she had slipped into her new role as Lauro's lover. She was accepted with no fuss—they were devoted to her.

Here, in the relaxed family holiday environment, the contrast between Lauro and his mother was most apparent. Where Lauro was essentially Italian, his mother was plain, tall, angular and spare, an American Gothic, splendid looking, rather unworldly, apart from society and worldly concerns, interested in things of the mind and spirit but not an intellectual as was her son. Her calm and dignity were in contrast to his ebullience and vitality. Mrs. Bailey Aldrich, who, as Elizabeth Perkins, knew Lauro in his 1926 Harvard summer, describes him:

> His radiant personality was so infectious that he transformed common-
> places into exciting new realities. He sometimes made me think of a
> bird who is so happy he cannot decide on which branch to settle. He
> opened my eyes, merely through his reactions to ordinary beauties
> and the mystery and possibilities of life. . . . We were horseback riding
> and after a steady canter were walking our horses through a beauti-
> ful trail. He suddenly turned to me, almost shouting with excitement,
> "Sing—sing something!" His unself-consciousness in expression was
> a joy to a New Englander! His expansive nature was contagious—how
> *alive* he was!

On August 2, Ruth sailed, with Lauro, on the SS *Augustus*, and went immedi-ately, with Harriet and Aileen, to Dark Harbor for a three-week holiday. Lauro came for a few days; it was his only visit there.

During Ruth's tour in December 1929, while she was in Chicago, there is the only recorded mention by Lauro of marriage. He wrote Ruth that he had talked with Ned Sheldon of his sudden desire for marriage, but they had concluded that there was little to be gained—unless she wished for a child. In another context, Ruth once remarked that she lacked the courage to have a child. In the event, they did not marry, and there is no written evidence that Lauro pushed the matter.

Lauro could be sure that he had Ruth's love because she was deeply, unreserv-edly in love. One had only to hear her speak his name—every vowel in L A U R O was given full value, "rolled on her tongue," said Laura White, "and when she spoke of Lauro something changed in her throat and her voice had a different note and timbre." In Ruth's love there was all innocence, freshness, and unvarying won-der. It was, to her, a holy thing. Like a Fundamentalist and Scripture, Lauro's word became, to her, The Word. Even so, Ruth recognized the historical and tempera-mental hazards to their marriage: that she was seventeen years older than he; the difference in their personal worlds—his Italian, intellectual, and literary and hers English-American, social, and musical, and her work on the international stage—none of which could she nor would she change or forego in any degree. Above all there was her "constitutional baulking at making any binding commitment." Years later, Neville Rogers, who came to know the de Bosis family in 1944 when he was a Royal Air Force (RAF) intelligence officer in Rome, and came to know Ruth in

1946 and to whom she spoke a great deal of Lauro and of their love, said: "My guess is that Ruth and Lauro never knew quite what they wanted. She often said to me, 'I never was quite sure that I really understood Lauro; you understand him so much better than I.'" Running always through Ruth's relationships was this note of humility—this low estimate of her own worth.

Again in 1930, Ruth spent six weeks visiting the de Bosis family. It was during this time that she did the only painting she is known to have done. It is a very creditable, small oil painting of the shore and headland of Mt. Conéro, on which the Torre di Portonovo is situated.

Together she and Lauro returned to New York on October 13. He planned to resign his position as executive secretary of the Italy-America Society and to secure an appointment as representative in Italy of the Institute for International Education. He had come to a fork in the road, a decisive and daring change of direction. Like many young Italians, Lauro at first admired Mussolini's strong leadership. The political, social, and economic situation in Italy in 1922 had been extremely complex, well beyond the comprehension of the King, whose delay in taking the necessary action permitted Mussolini's assumption of government control. Fascism, feeding on its own power, shortly was revealed in all its ruthless force by the murder, for speaking out against the regime, of the Socialist deputy Giacomo Matteotti in June 1924. Obviously the government was implicated, and obviously the trial was rigged. But again the King could not bring himself to take decisive action. Inhibited by their fear of a political reaction that would bring the Communists into power, the Italians lost their last chance to restore a rule of law and order and justice.

At the time of the Matteotti murder, Lauro had been preoccupied with an interview for an extensive and diverse lecture tour in the United States, under the auspices of the Italy-America Society, and then was absorbed in the preparation of a group of twenty lectures on Italian history and culture. At this time, his father, Adolfo de Bosis, suffering a lingering and painful illness, died on August 24. Lauro, though moved by the Matteotti murder, still had no real political focus. The de Bosis family was not politically minded, and the full implications of Fascism, so far outside Lauro's experiences, had yet to sway him.

His eight-month lecture book tour took Lauro right across the United States. For the first time, he was exposed to an open press and could talk with some of the more important Italian political exiles, notably Count Carlo Sforza, the ex-prime minister, and Gaetano Salvemini. He began to see the reality beneath the Fascist rhetoric and bombast. On his return, he began to understand the brutality and tyranny of Fascist totalitarianism. In July 1926, as a lecturer at the Harvard Summer School, he spoke further with the exiles, particularly Giorgio La Piana, a Catholic Modernist and professor of church history at Harvard, who was a vocal and committed anti-Fascist.

Now, in June 1930, Lauro determined that he would do what he could to alert educated Italian men and prepare a group to take over political control when the regime fell—as he was sure it shortly would—even thinking of the role he, himself, might play in a new order. For Lauro, a follower of Benedetto Croce, the supreme crime of Fascism was the betrayal of the Risorgimento (a period of cultural nationalism and political unification), and he longed for Italy to return to the days of Cavour and Mazzini—who now took their place in his gallery of heroes. He was an idealist, a novice, totally without experience in political let alone clandestine activities. He worked entirely alone and in secret, confiding in no one. He was certain that if he could inform a sufficient number of intelligent, prominent men, the Truth, in their hands, could bring down the regime.

Beginning on July 1, Lauro mailed the first of a bimonthly series of newsletters containing excerpts from the most responsible foreign press as well as factual analyses of Fascist statements. He sent his newsletter to six hundred prominent Italians, with the request that each one forward copies to six like-minded men. He called his scheme the Alleanza Nazionale. There were similar newsletters being circulated by other groups, and, together, they must have been having some effect, for Mussolini ordered their ruthless suppression.

Lauro completed his plans in New York and sailed on November 26 for England, en route to Rome. Just before his ship reached England, on the 30th, his mother was arrested. A few days earlier, two friends, enlisted at the last moment to cover for him while out of the country, had been arrested while posting the mid-November newsletter. The police found, under his mother's bed, the duplicating machine used in making the six hundred copies.

Ruth, in Boston, staying with Esther Pickman, learned of the arrests from Giorgio La Piana on Monday, December 1, just before a dinner party and her opening night. "She was stunned, she turned dead white, I thought she would faint," said Matilda Pfeiffer. "But she said 'I can't talk of it now but immediately after the performance I must go to a cable office to wire Lauro not to cross the frontier.'" With the iron discipline of her stagecraft, Ruth got through the dinner and her performance. As soon as she was rid of her congratulatory visitors, she rushed to send a wire, which Lauro received on his arrival the next morning.

Lauro's immediate reaction was to proceed at once by train to Rome to take responsibility for the activities of his mother and friends, but a telephone call from Romolo Ferlosio, a family friend outside the circle of suspicion, advised him not to return but to meet with him in Bern, in Switzerland, the next day. Lauro proceeded accordingly and for two weeks met with colleagues and received messages from his sister, Charis, and Vittorio, his brother. All urged him *not* to return to certain imprisonment, possibly even death. It would do no good and only add to the trouble and anxiety of his family. Better he remain outside Italy to continue his work.

He was persuaded and returned to Paris to await the verdict of the trial of his mother and two friends. He hoped to be tried *in absentia* and to be condemned; that, he felt, would be a feather in his cap and of great value if he should do a lecture tour in America.

Ruth wrote to Giorgio La Piana that a cable had come from Vittorio de Bosis to relatives in New York saying, "All settled mother splendid." She went on: "I pray Lauro will do nothing rash though he means to continue the work. Do warn him to 'go slow' for if they find he is still working he will be in grave danger and they may make it harder for his mother and friends. His return to Italy would be a futile sacrifice now and I hope he will not be tempted by sentiment to do anything rash." She added: "I am anxious not to be known as a close friend of the family in case at some time it could help to have me go to Italy."

In Rome, Signora de Bosis was persuaded by a Fascist lawyer—the only person permitted to talk with her—that her children were in jail and Lauro's friends free and that if she wrote a letter of apology to Mussolini for her anti-Fascist actions and pledging her loyalty in the future, there would be no trial and everything would be dissolved. Swayed by concern for her family and with the utmost reluctance, knowing full well that she would forever feel the shame and dishonor of abandoning her stand for freedom, she wrote the letter. On December 22 a trial was held, her letter was read, and the charges against her were dismissed. But to her astonishment and chagrin, she found Lauro's two friends, Mario Vinciguerra and Renzo Rendi, on trial and sentenced to fifteen years in prison. Her children had not been accused and all were free. Lauro, to his humiliation, was ignored and discredited.

Ruth was frantic with worry and again wrote La Piana:

> It was a great shock and disappointment to me and their friends that she did not abide by her confession and 'denied her faith' so to speak but I suppose the pressure was terrific; probably the family were frightened to death by threats and warnings and no doubt Mussolini's physician, Puccinelli, brought pressure to bear, being their great friend and Vittorio's chief. I feel if she had remained silent she might have got free, and not perhaps have brought such terrible judgment on those two men. Still, one never knows just what the situation was. Do write Lauro and warn him to 'go slow.' I feel he is too optimistic and impetuous. His motive, of course, is fine—but I don't think he reckons with the terrific power of the police and spy system and the awful fear which paralyses even those in sympathy with the cause. I cannot think the country is really aroused and ready yet and if it was—who is to be the leader? O, it's all so tragic and I feel premature—but it is a gallant effort and no doubt has done some good. I hear from other sources that Mussolini was terrified and furious and deeply disturbed. I believe Lauro is continuing the pamphlets from Paris; I feel he is in great danger there and that London would be safer from every point of view. He should take every precaution for the good of the cause, and if he continues to infuriate the authorities Paris is the easiest place to play some dastardly trick to get him over the border or do away with him. Perhaps, if you agree in this, you would write to that effect. I am sure he is in an exalted state of mind and that Paris is a sinister and dangerous atmosphere also for excited tem-

peramental natures! London is sobering and more healthful for normal growth and activity I think! . . . If you or the Pfeiffers can think
of any way of sending money to the Rendi family and the little
Vinciguerra girl, do let me know—it is going to be difficult, I fear.
. . . Forgive this long letter but it is a comfort to talk to you.

This was Ruth's first experience of political action, of clandestine opposition;
and, however right her instincts, it was an area completely foreign to her knowledge and sense of reality. "A year ago," Lauro pointed out to her, she "had not been
interested in Fascism so now it seems a terrible increase in distress."

Warily, Lauro made contact with a few other exiled anti-Fascists: Nitti, a former
prime minister, Gioacchino Dolci, Luigi Sturzo in London, Francesco Luigi Ferrari
in Brussels. But he remained as inconspicuous as possible. Ruth was frantic with
worry. She wanted to cancel all her engagements at once to be with him in Paris.
She sent money, which he refused for himself or his family but deposited in an
account "for future work" such as the publication of the collection of his bimonthly
letters. "I will freely write you," he promised. "There are many important things
that may be done later on and which will badly need help." She sent boxes of food,
which, he protested, were not needed. She sent a "Rolls Royce of typewriters" so
that he could get on with the books he "burned to write."

During January, February, and March, he wrote repeatedly to reassure her, to
quiet her fears and beg her not to come. He was "prepared to a long exile." Again
he said, "Do not come, do everything as if I did not exist. We must be *extremely*
cautious. Achieve your plans as if nothing had happened. Do not come." Ruth
could not understand why she should not join him. Was there a flaw in her love?
Why should Lauro be fearful of attracting attention to her, of further attracting
"the unfavorable voices" by which he felt surrounded? George La Piana wrote him
a long, reasoned letter, very critical of the effective wisdom of his activities.

Ruth was in no sense an ideologue and not one to take up arms for a "cause,"
much as she deplored tyranny, violence, lack of freedom—all that Fascism represented. While many have spoken of Ruth Draper's support of anti-Fascist work
and her involvement in the struggle against it, it must be realized that her "involvement and support" were *not* at the level of the "Cause," however much she
supported its ideal, but at the personal level of her love for Lauro de Bosis. She
had no confidence in his activity—she took no action herself—and would have
given a great deal to dissuade him from these activities for which he had no training or experience and was, basically, unfitted. She did not believe his actions wise
or constructive but, in her humility and love, could not steel herself to really em-
phatic efforts to turn him in another direction—even had that been possible.
Throughout his life, Lauro had complete assurance in his own ideas and deter-
minations and went his own way no matter what other judgments might be presented to him.

Sixteen years earlier, in quite another context, Ruth had written to Dorothea:
"The strange inhibition to mingle in affairs that has always kept me merely a suf-

fering onlooker, instead of an active helpful party, possesses me now as always."
Now, in 1931, it possessed her still.

Clearly, Lauro did not need the daily concern and care Ruth's presence would
mean. He had taken a job as concierge of the Hôtel Victor Emmanuel III and
was completely absorbed in his "great dream." He had said, "I will have no peace
until the struggle comes to an end." He would learn to pilot, secure an airplane,
and fly over Rome at dusk to drop anti-Fascist letters to the King and to the citi-
zens of Rome. In this way, he hoped—even expected—to alert them to the lies of
Fascism and to urge quite legal actions that, in his opinion, would contribute to
the downfall of the regime. The experienced flyers whom he consulted stressed
the need for many hours of training and all urged that he not pilot the plane himself—he was too valuable to the "Cause" to risk his life in this fashion—surely
the Fascist air force would shoot down his unarmed "little bird." But Lauro would
not listen. He made and remade plans. He talked with the men who had made a
similar flight over Milan in July 1930. He was consumed by envy—he "must do
the same for the *Alleanza Nazionale*." He was completely carried away by the
romantic daring of this great gesture that would redeem his honor and that of his
mother. He was determined to go, and to go alone. No argument could persuade
him otherwise. He would become a hero, a symbol. He raised sufficient funds from
his anti-Fascist colleagues also in exile in England and Belgium. He arranged for
instruction and took a physical examination. He gave up his job as concierge at
the Hôtel Victor Emmanuel III.

On April 14 Ruth arrived in Paris. She had, with reluctance and in constant
anxiety, carried out engagements in New York, Washington, and Boston, as well
as in Canada; she was booked for a spring season in Paris and for her usual London season in June. Lauro met her boat train and, the next day, in her suite at the
Hotel Lancaster, told her of his plan. "After the first shock she was wonderful and
never said one word to deter me." However, she wrote to Harriet: "I feel so far
off from the vision he sees—so unequal—so unworthy."

Lauro began his flying lessons at Toussus-le-Noble, near Versailles, and made
his first solo flight on May 24. That night Ruth completed three very successful
weeks performing for French audiences. Then Lauro went underground—his plan
had been betrayed to the Fascists. Ruth crossed to London, again to the small house
at 28 Chapel Street, near Belgrave Square, and opened on June 6 for a four-week
season. Lauro joined her for a few days at a time.

From June 28 to July 11, Lauro received instruction from Owen Cathcart-
Jones, who strongly advised against the flight. He told this writer that "Lauro was
a novice, temperamentally too excitable for a really reliable pilot." Assuredly, the
Italian air force would shoot him down, but he had the determination and he had
the airplane, a de Haviland "Moth." As indicated in his letters, both Dr. Sicca in
London and d'Arsac in Brussels had contributed generously to its purchase. The
opinion that Ruth bought it for him is, therefore, not substantiated. She did, in
fact, pay for the flying lessons in England—"by cheque through Morgan's Bank
in New York," said Cathcart-Jones.

Lauro was obsessed. No matter that he had flown solo for only five hours; after he had dropped his letters, it would not matter if he did not return, his mission would have been accomplished. Nothing could deter him. He was completely caught up in his d'Annunzian vision of the redemptive value of the heroic deed, of honor reclaimed.

In apprehension and anguish, Ruth returned to Paris on the 11th to the Hotel Lancaster to wait while Lauro made his attempt. She heard nothing until the 14th—a telegram said the flight was "put off." On July 13, Cathcart-Jones had flown the "Moth" from England to Cannes, where, on a beautiful sunny afternoon, Lauro met him. In his excitement, Lauro loosed his letters in a breeze. Frantically, they were collected, and Lauro took off for Corsica to refuel. On landing in a field, one wing was so severely damaged that the "Moth," with its load of letters, had to be abandoned. His plan now revealed, Lauro fled to Switzerland, as the French police would be looking for him. Hastily packing a suitcase, Ruth joined him at the Ernest Schellings, on Lake Geneva. Now she, too, went underground, and for many weeks, her family at home knew nothing of her whereabouts. Only Aileen, in Paris, knew, and Harriet, and the Kochanskis, who were nearby in Switzerland. "I never dreamed there was such hell as I have known and know I must go through it—and maybe worse—again."

While Lauro left for Munich in search of another plane, Ruth returned to Paris to collect her luggage and to consult, in Lauro's behalf, with Salvemini. Lauro found a plane in Munich, a Messerschmitt, for which he would pay, it was reported, eight thousand francs. It has been widely assumed that Ruth Draper financed this second airplane. There is no firm proof either that she did or that she did not; her canceled checks and bank statements for 1931 no longer exist. As she was very careful with money and was strongly opposed to the flight, it is questionable that however great her devotion, she would totally fund an enterprise that Lauro's moneyed colleagues were unwilling to further support. However, she may have provided the final segment of the purchase price, thus making the flight possible, although Salvemini said d'Arsac paid for the plane.

Delayed by mechanical problems, Ruth and Lauro now set off on a "bicycling" in the Black Forest and Bavarian Alps. The situation was taking its toll of Ruth's nervous energy: guilty because she could not communicate with her family; the constant movement because Salvemini said they should not stay long in any one place—where Ruth was, Lauro was likely to be also; her mounting and justifiable fears regarding Lauro's activities and plan, in which she could not believe. It was almost more than she could endure. Finally, she wrote Harriet: "If anything should ever happen to me—I think I'd like my sisters to know—from you and Aileen and Zosia [Kochanski]—how happy I've been and how perfect was the love we had."

There was more delay. Mechanical failures of the ejector for his letters, illness of those who had promised to help, miscarriage of letters, fears of detection, bad weather—all added to her fears and nearly exhausted patience. Again she wrote to Harriet: "He is confident, courageous and calm. I am terrified. I hope I do not regret what I've done."

At last Lauro went to Marseilles to meet the German pilots who were bringing the Messerschmitt on September 7. The date passed. She walked the floor all night, several nights—no word came. Then a delayed telegram came saying that it was necessary that the plane return to Munich for adjustments to the ejector. Lauro returned to Geneva to await the next dark of the moon. Then for ten days they journeyed slowly through Talloires, Chambery, and Annecy, picking up an additional package of letters in Annemasse. Quickly then, via Avignon, they reached Marseilles by train on the afternoon of Friday, October 2. On the station platform, at four o'clock, they parted. Ruth continued on to Cannes, where she would spend that night with her friends, the French painter Lucien Monod and his American wife, nee Charlotte Todd McGregor of Milwaukee.

That evening, from the Hotel Terminus, Lauro posted a letter to her saying that the German pilots had telephoned, all was well, and they would arrive early the next morning. "I have still on my lips the perfume of yours, and if I close my eyes I feel you so close as if I might hold you in my arms. I think I could live 100 years on the sweetness accumulated these days. What a bewitcher you are! . . . I found everything all right and burn to go and be through with this thing. I feel absolutely sure of this success and am not even excited about it. It has become almost a matter of 'routine.' I embrace you with redoubled ardor and tenderness." In a note on her handwritten copy of the letter, Ruth added: "He was wonderfully patient and calm, tho' inwardly restless and eager to get it over with. His reference to 'routine' and not being excited was partly to lessen my fears, and also because he'd started and been held up so many times."

From his childhood, Lauro had been in thrall to the legendary heroes of mythology, enraptured by the classical Greek poets, with the cult of Shelley, and with the flamboyant romanticism of D'Annunzio—his father's boyhood friend whom his mother thought "outrageous." The "hero" had become an obsession. An American woman, his mother's close friend, said of Lauro, "The daemon of the hero was ever at his elbow." He was in thrall, now, to his own vision, his "great dream," his gesture of redemption. At the start of his planning, he intended to return from Rome, to make other flights, and, "with this prestige to make a triumphant lecture tour in America." But somewhere, late in the long months of exile, in lonely introspection, he had come to believe that his flight might be received as merely a *beau geste*, but that if his life was given, then his message would carry conviction. "It is necessary to die," he wrote this night before his flight. "Fascism will not end until some twenty young people sacrifice their lives in order to awaken the spirit of the Italians. . . . I shall be worth more dead than alive." He felt that the unhappiness of the dozen people nearest him, while tragic, was far outweighed by the "happiness or unhappiness of 42 million Italians." Torn by grief and remorse that his friends, not he, were in jail, by the shame of his mother's letter to Mussolini, by his own discrediting, he believed that by his flight and probable death, his "life would be justified."

By this time he appears to have given little thought to his return flight and, it appears, made no preparation for refueling in Corsica on his way back. Actually, he expected to be shot down. In his mind, he was to become one more martyr of anti-Fascism. Salvemini knew this, and Dolci, among others. But Ruth, in all her anguished apprehension, believed that if all went well, he could and would return.

During the night at the hotel, Lauro wrote, by hand, in French, his testament, "The Story of My Death." He also wrote a "last letter" to Ruth. These he sent to his friend Ferrari in Brussels, with instructions that if he was captured or did not return, the letter be forwarded to Ruth in care of Leá Dessay in Paris and the testament released to the press. He would telegraph from Nice on his return. He posted these on his way to the airfield at Marignane early the next afternoon. That morning, Saturday, Ruth left for Paris. Lauro and Salvemini thought it best that she wait there in Leá's apartment at No. 65 Avenue Wagram. Salvemini would be in Paris, too, and Aileen Tone and Lugné-Poe, and she would be near other friends in Paris and London.

Two German flyers brought the Messerschmitt to Marignane. Lauro had told them that he would fly to Barcelona with advertising matter, so they fueled the plane for a flight of that length. They filled only one reserve tank. This left him short of fuel for the flight he actually would make: Marseilles to Rome to Corsica plus maneuvers over Rome. Lauro had had only seven and a half hours of solo flight experience, he had not flown for several weeks, and this would be the longest sustained flight he had yet attempted. At 3:15 (4:15 Rome time in 1931), he took off; he arrived over Rome about 8:00. It was a clear twilight, and the streets and cafés were crowded. Gliding in silently over the city, Lauro suddenly, at full throttle, circled, dove, and swooped low over the rooftops, widely scattering four hundred thousand small, thin-paper letters—to the King and to the people of Rome. Because the packets of letters were dropped from so low a height, many of them did not burst open and were the more easily collected by the police. But in many places the ground and people in the open-air cinema were thickly covered by a white blizzard. After thirty or forty minutes, the plane rose and disappeared toward the west. Lauro's surprise had been complete.

Ruth waited with Leá, walking the floor—"Pense tu—il est en train de vol?"—beside herself with fear and anxiety and apprehension. She was exhausted but could not rest. No word came. Sunday morning, still no word. She stayed by the telephone—no call, no telegram. She telephoned to Aileen Tone, who came at once. Salvemini was there and Leá's friend, Dr. Bardi. On Tuesday the flight was reported in the press, which said that the Italian air force had pursued the flier. Nothing more was known. There were no claims that the flier had been shot down. On the 7th, Ruth received Lauro's farewell letter. He said:

Be happy for my sake! Not only proud but *happy.* You wanted me to play a role in the life of my country. I can assure you that not even in 50 years of successful work I could have attained such a role. Wait and see! Not right away but I will become a symbol and achieve 100

71

times more this way than if I were alive. . . . You have made my life a real paradise for over three years. Don't make me now the injustice of rendering me a cause of sadness. I am happy. Be happy. 'Sta allegra' and work. You will have given me then your crowning boon. If you do that I will feel that my love continues after death to protect you, otherwise my soul would never have peace. Never until you are again happy. And *please* love somebody else, I will consider [it] indirectly as love to me. I embrace you with all my adoration.

Lauro.

At her death, Ruth left a green leather letter-case, locked, containing Lauro's letters to her: a total of sixty-nine items—original signed, handwritten letters and ten telegrams; also his two final letters of October 2 and 3—not the originals but copies in Ruth's handwriting. The case was not to be opened until ten years after her death. She gave permission for the letters to be printed "if a serious book is written about L. de B."

On October 6, Ferrari released Lauro's testament, "The Story of My Death." It was printed on October 14 in *The Times* of London, in *The Manchester Guardian*, *The New York Times*, *Le Soir* of Brussels, and various other European newspapers. It ran largely uncut. In fact, *The New York Times* correspondent did not cable the story until he received assurance that it would be run in full. It has been said that Ruth made the English translation.

Leá's house and Ruth herself were under surveillance by Italian agents, and, one may be sure, the French police watched them off. It is probable that the telephone was tapped.

On Tuesday the 6th, Bill Carter, Ruth's nephew, arrived in Paris en route to the Institute of International Studies in Geneva. In a café, over coffee and croissants, he read with astonishment, in *The Times*, of Lauro's flight. By now it was reported that the Englishman "Sir Adolf Morris," as the German pilots knew him, was actually an Italian named Lauro de Bosis. When Bill went to Morgan's (Bank) to change some money, by good chance, he met Aileen Tone. "At Leá's," said Aileen. He went straight there and found Ruth in bed, exhausted, emotionally drained, prostrated by grief, desperate for eyewitness news from Rome.

Already Ruth had thought of sending Leá to learn what she could, to see Signora de Bosis, if possible. But Bill, suddenly available, unknown to the police in Rome, would not be recognized as her nephew and, above all, would not be under the eye of the French police. Salvemini agreed and, taking a silver pencil case from his watch chain, removed the pencil and inserted the names and addresses of four men whom Bill should try to talk with—but in the greatest secrecy and with the utmost caution and wariness. Feeling rather "cloak and daggerish," Bill arrived in Rome in the early evening of October 10 and set off at once. He found Monsieur Lattes at home, and they talked with all doors closed against the ears of his servant. M. Lattes knew little but would try to meet Umberto Zanotti-

Bianco, casually, in a corridor: "He is followed everywhere and one never uses his tapped telephone to arrange an appointment." The next morning Bill met with Miss Cohen of the American Library, a friend of Signora de Bosis's, to give her a letter to be passed on at her discretion. She was deaf, nervous, and very frightened. Through her, Bill met with M. de Masi, who knew Lauro well, had been on the streets at the time of the flight, and had noticed people in the crowd quietly shoving the letters into their pockets. He said the effect was electric: "Coming into the square was like coming into a new world"—something he had not felt for years. There was astonishment, he said, and admiration for the sheer daring and skill of the pilot, and praise for the educated simplicity of the letters. It was said that Mussolini was "hopping mad"—Lauro had not only breached Italian security but also "buzzed" the Palazzo Chigi, where Mussolini was working. He had immediately ordered "spontaneous" demonstrations, with many motorcycles.

That afternoon, M. de Lattes took Bill to see Zanotti-Bianco. "Up and down stairs, through little rooms, to a small sanctum where he sat behind his desk. There was no telephone, which surely would have been wired to pick up conversations in its area." They were reasonably safe, but Zanotti-Bianco suggested that they speak in French, rather than Italian or English. He confirmed the effect of the flight as, psychologically, a complete success and the outwitting of the air force as remarkable. Already the searchlight defense was noticeably reinforced and hard at work in practice. He said that Vinciguerra, in prison, was in better conditions. He said that if the Fascists had downed Lauro or captured him, they would proclaim it loudly. There was no clue. Apparently he had got clear away, but there were many rumors as to the direction he took, rumors of all kinds. He would try to find out more.

Wary and apprehensive on the train back to Paris, after forty hours in Rome, Bill returned, without incident, to report to Ruth and Salvemini.

Under a Marseilles dateline of October 8, Reuters reported: "There is still no news of the missing flyer who dropped pamphlets over Rome. He is believed to have deliberately thrown away his life after dropping the leaflets by steering his machine out over the sea to Corsica, well knowing that there was not enough fuel to take him there."

On the 6th, the press reported, the prefect of Corsica had ordered a complete search of the island, and the French naval authorities at Toulon were sending out gunboats to search the sea; it was feared that Lauro had run out of fuel before reaching Corsica. Airplanes in the area also kept a sharp lookout for his wooden plane or any trace of wreckage.

Salvemini, "so proud and full of tenderness" that it comforted Ruth, came daily, and Dr. Bardi came every day for breakfast and the last thing at night, bringing wisdom and his clear point of view. "Lugné like a rock—keen to protect me from any possible annoyance of police or papers—he is wise and kind, he *is* such a fine friend." Aileen was with her. Amey Aldrich and Jane and Wilfred de Glehn and Philip Monod came. There was a great deal for her to do, going through Lauro's papers, trying to get word through to his family, and working to have articles written and published about Lauro and his ideals. She began to function as his widow. She would, of course, not be permitted to cross the Italian frontier, but various people carried communications back and forth for her. Ruth's energy, she found, "was being alarmingly spent in the first terrible days of shock."

The Paris press reported that Morgan and Company was holding a forty thousand dollar reward for information as to Lauro's whereabouts; a reward of five thousand dollars had been posted "by an Englishwoman" for any solid information; and an unknown English-speaking woman had hired a plane on the Riviera and spent several days searching the sea in the area of Sardinia.

Ruth had no desire to go home: "My only comfort is to be near friends who knew and cared for him. At home I'd feel so cut off from sympathy with his ideals. I think I'll just stay on here; I feel no desire to move—I feel arrested—afraid to touch the earth—afraid, really, to hope." Rumors were rife: Lauro was being hidden in Yugoslavia, in Sardinia, in Algiers, in Corsica; he had been picked up by a ship and unable to communicate; since no trace of his plane had been found, possibly he was alive.

On November 30, Ruth wrote a letter to George La Piana, asking his help in having articles published. Then she added: "Lauro and I would have been married had he returned." She did not mail this letter; the original is among her papers, and no variation of it exists in the La Piana papers at Harvard. This is the only mention so far discovered that she and Lauro might have married. Perhaps in the tense emotion of those long summer months, she may have come to believe she would marry him. But one cannot escape some doubt as to her actually doing so. There is no evidence that in their hearts they really wanted marriage. In her many very frank talks with Neville Rogers, a determination to marry was never mentioned. Existing letters to Harriet Marple contain no mention of the decision. In conclusion to La Piana, Ruth said, "I, of course, would not wish any publicity about this, but I feel I should like you and the Pfeiffers to know." Matilda Pfeiffer, in long talks with this writer, said she had believed they would not marry and, herself, thought it would be most unwise: "We all think if Ruth marry Lauro she would be *very* disappointed." In a letter to Harriet—dated March 28, 1934—Ruth wrote: "I know I'm too selfish and too cowardly ever to make any decision that involves sacrifice."

A quick visit to London in December was necessary in order to make arrangements for a tour of the smaller English cities and also to help with the settling of von zur Mühlen's estate. Ruth knew his affairs were in disorder and a few months earlier had written: "The bill for doing over and replacing [Master's] furniture amounts to 1200 odd pounds!!! The furniture company wrote and asked *me* to be the guarantor, before they would deliver it. I refused. It's really serious and a bit staggering. I'm just putting in a bathroom for him in the Round House and pay him nearly 300 pounds a year besides—and now this bill—it's a bit thick! But of course I won't agree to be responsible." She returned to Paris for Christmas with Aileen and Harriet. She received a letter of one sentence from Edith Wharton: "Dear Mifs Draper, I know the heartbreak and I know the emptiness. Yours ever, Edith Wharton." With it she enclosed a copy of her poem "In a Library"—hitherto unknown and written, possibly, at the time of Walter Berry's death; she had inherited many of his books.

> If you were dead should I still feel you near,
> Mixed with all daily happiness as the light
> Is with the air, the sea, the budding year,
> And blackthorn turning all the lanes to white?
> Should I say at every turn: He's here?
>
> If death be changing, you can never die,
> While what you are still warms me to the soul,
> While everything I look at, to my eye
> Is but half seen till yours has made it whole,
> And over all my earth you bend your sky?
>
> If death be easing, then you are not dead.
> Your hand is on the latch, your happy call
> Rouses the house, and your impatient tread—
> And sometimes, in the quiet of day's fall
> Walking the empty rooms with my old pain,
> Among your books I find you with bent head,
> And, o my soul, our lips are one again.

Mrs. Wharton invited Ruth to her winter home, Sainte Claire le Château in Hyères on the Mediterranean, for a rest and change. Berenson would be there, as he frequently was, for a Christmas visit, as well as Gaillard Lapsley, an Anglicised American and don of Trinity College in Cambridge, and also the English painter, Robert Norton—Berenson called them "Edith's male wives." Usually chatty and charming, this year they were morose and uncommunicative, and B. B. found them tiresome. Ruth did not accept the invitation but, at his urging, wrote B. B. there. On December 30, B. B. replied:

> Thank you for your beautiful letter. It is so beautiful that I long to show it to friends in Italy and yet I dare not send it by post or carry it. That is the measure of the freedom we enjoy. All my acquaintances are marked, and subject to having our correspondence opened and, if Italians, to be subject to domiciliary visits and parquisitions.
>
> You ask how long it will last. Neither the middle nor upper classes show the least sign of caring for personal liberty as distinct from independence of foreign rule. The Italian has never known what personal freedom was, nor has he, since Dante, known indignation over

certain aspects of conduct. Of course I know there are exceptions. Was not *he* one of them?

I remember seeing you together looking at Bonfigli's "Nativity" in my bedroom and I understood it all. Every time I saw you since, I longed to talk to you about him and you. Now you have him forever. No, my heroic soul, it never passed through my heart or mind to pity you. I may be a bad soul but I am not a small soul, and am humbly capable of understanding you. And understanding I approve what you mean to do, and your attitude toward memory and toward life. No, I don't pity, I envy you. You have lived, you have seen as few. And who can take it away from you!

He asked her to write to him, in Settignano, about herself and signing "Ruth." He signed himself, "Your affectionate and devoted friend. B. B."

By early January, Marie Curtis had been to Italy to see Lauro's mother, with gifts from Ruth, photographs of Lauro, and things that were his. Most important was a letter giving the details for which she longed and which only Ruth could tell her. There were gifts, also, for Elena and her children. Marie brought back a long letter, dated December 20, from "Caramadre" to Ruth:

My darling blessed Ruth,

I cannot tell you how deeply I feel the dear letter you sent me by M. It is balm to know that you two had those beautiful weeks in the summer, to strengthen and bless him, to sweeten your bitter cup. His was a perfect life, but without you and all that you gave him it would never have reached that height, nor have been complete. I am unspeakably grateful to you and I love you in a way I cannot describe. I hope you will understand. I know you will. . . .

Later I shall feel the pride more fully. Now I must slowly become accustomed to the severing. But perhaps I shall never realize it. I have not given up hope. A spark remains and will burn until positive proof comes—or at least for a long time yet.

Nothing matters but that we are proud and grateful, and that we love you. Mostly I think of what those last hours of flight must have held for him of triumph, poetry, exaltation. Valente [another son, who fell into the sea from his seaplane in 1919], Shelley, the beauty of the earth, the sea, the night—solitude, harmony. Perhaps—he was content to end life so.

And a letter from Elena, dated January 2, 1932:

My dear dear Ruth,

You know that all the time our thoughts are with you. . . . Never should we have lived to see his death—beautiful as he has known how to make it—we are left without our pride and our love and our youth and everything that made our family bright—what can ever console us? There is no consolation. We shall cry bitterly when we feel weak but also often, as he taught us, strengthen ourselves in the pride of what he did, rejoice at the beauty of his death and at the supreme joy he felt—to be happy as he so often was and as he would have liked everyone to be is no more possible—he was a beloved child to each of us.

All our thoughts of love, your Elena

The de Bosis family lived in anxiety and uncertainty. Money was short and there was little even for local travel. They were not sure what to do. They lived quietly, attracting no attention, minimizing their association with friends so as not to endanger them also. Friends from other countries were careful when visiting Italy not to try to see any of the family unless asked to do so. When Nancy Cox MacCormack came to Rome in the fall of 1931, she sent word, discretely, to Percy de Bosis, Lauro's eldest brother, who came to her hotel and sat talking with her in a small reception room. His surveillance "watcher" followed him in and sat nearby plainly listening to their conversation. For a reserved, nonpolitical family, these were desperately trying and tragic times.

Elena Vivante and Vittorio, both of whom adored Lauro, understood his motivation more sympathetically than the others; there was considerable tension in the family relationships. Vittorio, a fine surgeon in the hospital in Florence, knew well that advancement in his career was now shadowed and that even his job might be in some danger, a serious loss, perhaps, in his responsibilities toward his mother. He tried to protect her from further anguish, and she came to Florence to be with him and Elena for rest and comfort. The eldest daughter, Virginia, a brilliant linguist and Arabic scholar, with her husband, Giovanni Vacca, a great Chinese scholar and professor, were undoubtedly apprehensive as to the security of their government-controlled university positions. Virginia felt bitterly that Lauro's anti-Fascist activities were willful, misguided, thoughtless of his family, and, inexperienced and untrained as he was, had been a terrible misfortune, putting them all at risk. She and Ruth never met. Vittorio thought that Lauro never really saw their situation as it was. In May he wrote to Ruth:

> It has been impossible for me to write—mentally impossible—to you or to anybody I love. But you have been and you are always near my heart. My love and devotion is beyond words, and even the sad side of your remembrance is dear to my soul. Everybody at home feels the same way, and the only reason we don't rush to see you is that there is no chance of getting a passport.
>
> Mother went through many terrible moments and many times her hopes have been raised by vague news or rumours that made her hope

again. She is beautifully strong and brave—ready to hear any tragic definite news and thinking that *logically* there is *no* hope whatsoever.

Dear, dear Ruth! You can't imagine what you mean to us and how I love you.

V.

Ruth belonged to them as they, to her, became "my family in Italy." She took them very seriously, with an abiding and tender concern. But she never shared them with her own family. *This* relationship was separate and apart—this was hers alone, ever held close to her heart.

For months, various "crank" letters came to Signora de Bosis, some even purporting to be from Lauro. It was a cruel time. It became obvious, too, that the Regime had no firm solution to Lauro's disappearance. When early in 1932 a young English woman of Spanish blood and distinctly Italian appearance, who was employed as governess at the Vivantes' Villa Solaia, went to Naples to meet her cousin arriving by ship from South America (a dark-haired young man also of Italian appearance), she was kept under close surveillance and, upon his arrival, both were arrested, imprisoned, and questioned—"grilled"—for several days. He was thought to be Lauro, until it was pointed out that he had blue eyes—whereas Lauro's eyes were known to be brown. Ruth herself continued occasionally to be watched, as she was well aware. However, the report made by its agents to the Fascist government stated that there was nothing offensive to the Italian State in her performance, that it was merely a rendition of well-known Italian types. Probably Fascist agents kept an eye on her activities and her association with anti-Fascists such as Salvemini. She felt that she should be wary. The de Bosis family in Italy remained under surveillance, with career opportunities closed to Lauro's brothers, until the fall of Fascism in 1945.

Ruth continued to send money and gifts to Vinciguerra's little daughter, who had over her bed the photograph of Lauro that Ruth had sent. She got money through, also, to the wife of Renzo Rendi, whose twin sons were now four years old, and who now had another child. All these children would remain in her thoughts and generosity. Although determined to go on with her work onstage, her main preoccupation—almost an obsession—for several years would be to ensure a wider knowledge and recognition of "Lauro's tragic and beautiful story." She wanted to bring out an edition in English of his verse drama *Icaro*, which had won the Olympic Prize for Poetry in Amsterdam in 1928 and in which he strangely foretold the manner of his own death. Neither Professor G. M. Trevelyan in Cambridge nor Benedetto Croce in Italy could undertake the translation—Ruth, finally, decided to do it herself.

A few days before her opening in Brighton on January 11, Ruth returned to England; she was booked for a series of twelve one-week engagements throughout Great Britain. It was some time before the routine of her work steadied her to any degree emotionally. Although a month later, from Manchester, she wrote:

"I'm in the traces of this work now and it seems natural to go on. I see I'm giving enormous pleasure." Also, she was making considerable money to restore her resources, so seriously depleted over the preceding six months.

Arthur Rubinstein's wedding to Aniela Mylnarski was a great joy. Ruth shopped with the bride, helped her to pack, and was a witness for her at the wedding. But Aniela found her stiff, for all her warmth, a dominating force of which she was always a little afraid, although loving and admiring Ruth.

Ruth returned on weekends to see Mrs. Yates Thompson. In London, also, were the Mudie sisters, Mary and Winifred and Constance. For fifty years, Mrs. Mudie and her daughters had wintered in Rome to escape the fogs of London. In Rome they became intimate friends of Aldolfo and Lillian de Bosis and of their young children, whose growth they had closely watched. Mr. Mudie had been the founder and owner of Mudie's Library and Bookshop in London, a friend and supporter of Mazzini and other exiles of the Risorgimento, whose home was a haven for them all. Lauro had sent to Mary Mudie a copy of the compilation of his clandestine letters; on February 14, she had responded by urging him to take more time to mature his thinking and his plans, to "formulate a solid plan of the structure [he] wished to build upon that [he] wished to tear down." It was a tactful, lucid, well-reasoned, and wise letter. Although he ignored her advice, Lauro kept Mary Mudie's letter, and Ruth found it among his papers; she wrote to Mary Mudie and enclosed a copy of the booklet about Lauro in the Italy To-Day series. The Mudies already knew of Ruth from Lillian and from Lauro, so Mary welcomed her on the 17th, when, bearing a large bunch of tall, white lilies, she called to tell them of Lauro and her love for him. The lilies, they felt, were a "fit emblem of the highest, purest and most unselfish spirit" they had ever known. For Ruth, the Mudies were an incomparable link with Lauro.

The Oxford University Press accepted Ruth's translation of *Icaro*, and Gilbert Murray would write the preface. Lauro's anthology, *The Golden Book of Italian Verse*, would be out in October. She went to Mrs. Yates Thompson for the Sunday and August Bank Holiday. It was time to go home. For the time being, she had done all she could for Lauro. But the turmoil, terror, and tragedy of the past seventeen months abroad could not so quickly be stilled; she could not yet face home and family and friends; there had to be some period of readjustment. Sailing in late August to Canada, Ruth reached Islesboro on September 3 to spend several weeks alone and did not arrive in New York until early October.

These solitary days with her memories were a restorative. She lived over the two perfect days there with Lauro in 1929, she thought of sailing with her brother Paul and with Lauro in her little boat, and she thought of and cherished all the intimate associations of the past years. The beauty, and the sameness of nature, held and steadied her.

This love affair of Ruth and Lauro seems to have been inevitable, their respective natures, the attraction of opposites: the *young* man, the older woman; the reserved New England spinster, the romantic, passionate Italian man; his search for fame and recognition, her position and glamour as an established artist. His eagerness for romance and her longing for it bridged the gap between their two cultures, between Ruth's rigid, scrupulous standards and Lauro's warm, even hot-blooded Latin nature. Could the intensity of their love have endured? Already it had run three and a half years. Could his fine Italian eye and fancy long be denied flirtatious appreciation of other lovely ladies, however casual the encounter? Had Ruth ever imagined that even for an instant, he had been less than totally faithful, said her nephew, Paul, "it would have destroyed her—utterly destroyed her—before she died." Lauro held her separate and apart, in her stellar orbit, almost, in his life, in isolation. But around her his life surely must have continued to revolve in its normal currents.

These had, for Ruth, been euphoric, rhapsodic years. In the only remaining scrap of a letter to him—marked "wear this page next your heart"—she expressed thankfulness for all he had given her, "to hold forever in my heart as my 'panache'—my reason of life, my glory and possession—your love. You have shown me such beauty as I did not know was possible. Such exalted, blazing purity and beauty and tenderness. You saved me and quickened my spirit to a new life. . . . To me you have from the first been utterly perfect."

She would never let go of the adoration, the idealization, the beauty of their love. But when it came to his self-determined duty—his duty to redeem his and his mother's honor; his duty to the Italian people in the face of overwhelming tyranny; his duty as a poet, as his father had taught him, to cry out against injustice—Lauro did not hesitate for an instant. He expected Ruth to go on with her life and work; he asked her to love someone else.

The particular beauty of his early death, as was pointed out to her, was that it made certain Lauro would remain forever young, ardent, and idealistic, forever gallant and heroic, and, above all, forever hers. The challenge of long years together was a challenge neither would have to face. Their love had been, and remained to her, a "brief but perfect love," and she carried its memory as her "panache" to ennoble her remaining days.

Massimo Salvadori, himself a hero of the anti-Fascist resistance, said:

> The death of Lauro de Bosis had been Ruth's deepest emotional experience. It did not change her life externally. It changed her internally. She was a remarkable woman. She became a great woman.
>
> de Bosis gave his life to tell Italians, to tell the world, that Fascism is wrong, that tyranny—whatever the colour and the justification—is always wrong. . . . Through Lauro de Bosis and her love, Ruth Draper became a participant in the unending tragedy . . . we call history.

Enduringly, Ruth, together with Lauro, live on in legend—on the shores of the Adriatic. The local people, around the tower, remembered them, after a few years, idealized and romanticized, not as real people whom they all knew, but as a fairy story—a story more real than memory or fantasy, which they speak of among themselves and tell to their children—a legend to be cherished over the generations.

7

Journeys and Wars

ON THE EDGE OF HER FIFTIETH YEAR, well established in life and as a stage presence, Ruth Draper focused the next six years on a series of worldwide journeys, performing in far-distant countries to sold-out houses, to audiences riveted by the characters she brought them. That they might not understand the language she spoke and had no knowledge of the characters she portrayed did not matter; they clearly understood the people she presented, the emotions that drove them, and what they were about. It was an amazing triumph.

In 1933, in a prelude to "really strange places," Ruth went with Aileen Tone to Morocco in late March. The weather was terrible. They wore every sweater and coat they had, but the souks, the color and movement, and the baby donkeys made the filth and cold worthwhile. In Marrakesh, dining with the Pasha, Ruth performed a few monologues, often wondering what he made of them.

These travels are best described in Ruth's own words as set forth in her *Letters* and will not, therefore, be recounted here, except for some recently discovered highlights. Her attitudes and reactions have their own voice.

Now, as in all the travels and tours throughout her career, Ruth literally saw the world through the eyes of a child. The adjectives of her youth remained the adjectives of her later years. By word of all who knew her, Ruth never really matured. "But had she grown up," said Mildred Dunnock, "she could no longer have created and performed her monologues." With all the veneer of sophistication that she would acquire over thirty years in ever-widening social circles in England and on the Continent, Ruth still did not lose her naivete. But she developed considerable shrewdness about people and became adept at not being put upon in spite of the vulnerability of her intense emotionalism.

Everyone wanted to meet Ruth Draper. Of those who achieved more than a casual "how-do-you-do," few penetrated beyond the public persona. With all her reticence and fame, she was delightful, charming, and elegantly simple. Men and women of prominence and accomplishment were enchanted; Ruth listened with total concentration and appreciation. What they "did" was, to her, "really quite wonderful," for it was usually outside her own range of knowledge. Bill Carter thought she "had more knowledge than she let on." She certainly had more knowledge and grace in writing and speaking than her limited formal education would have led one to expect. However, she listened and read well, and she had a "good ear."

While these were professional tours, they also were a therapy; the business of planning and arranging the schedule, although she had a manager, required her concentrated thought, living in the present. That they extended her horizons and confirmed the universality of her talent was to be expected. But they did more than that. These tours demonstrated the ease with which she moved from one country and culture to another, noting the variations, finding interest and—at least—amusement in life as it appeared, rejecting only that which did not meet her standard of integrity, human dignity, and beauty. These journeys confirmed her ability to be at home in the world, wherever her career and curiosity took her.

From a reading of her letters, it is clear that Ruth looked to Alice for an understanding of her emotional responses, sensitive and highly sentimental as she was. "Those last hours in New York ripped me to pieces—leaving you, more than the others. Be kind to yourself and don't get too tired, and take taxis, and Ovaltine before you go to sleep."

Now, with Alice going westward to China and Ruth sailing eastward to England and her South African tour, she wrote:

> Your loving little farewell letter was like a continuation of your warm embrace. I never felt so close, felt your love so strong and freely given as when you and I kissed good-bye. Bless you, my beloved sister— bless the quiet hours when you let me reveal my pain and my pride— and helped me by your reassurance that I have not failed since I lost the actual contact with Lauro's inspiring and ardent presence. Only at moments do I feel it burning within me—fleeting moments—but they renew my faith. One thing I know you must feel—as I do—as one sets forth on these journeys—that we carry them with us [Lauro and Ned]—and never again need say farewell. They are closer in loneliness, closer in distant places, and we can find much consolation in this, that when we miss them most, need them most, love them most, they are most close.
>
> You are so wonderful, the way you live above your sorrow—yet with it—but turning it into force, constructive and actual and unselfish.

(Alice's son, Ned, had died, tragically, in March 1932.)

On January 1, 1934, Ruth wrote to Harriet Marple: "What a price fate has asked us to pay for our happiness. At times I feel I can't bear it—still I'm thankful. I have never felt the need of what he gave me so much, it seems to me; I miss him more and more, and the struggle to live by what he stood for and showed me—is beyond me, and becomes more difficult. I sometimes think I shall not have to live much longer—that I have given my best. I should so hate to 'burn dim,' but that is the fate of most of us and I need not flatter myself, perhaps, that I shall be spared the common lot."

On December 1, traveling alone, Ruth sailed in eighteen days to Capetown, South Africa, making the long train journey straight up-country to Johannesburg, where she performed for two weeks. As the houseguest of Lord and Lady Clarendon, she spent Christmas at Government House in Pretoria. Then she worked her way south: one week each in Pretoria and Durban and a few days each in Pieter Maritzburg, East London, and Port Elizabeth. She arrived in Capetown at the end of January and performed for two weeks, then set off by air for Wadi Haifa, sightseeing along the way and performing in Salisbury, Nairobi, and Bulawayo. Predawn departures, coming down for all meals and for the night, an unscheduled grounding at a small guest house where she performed for her fellow passengers, all added to her interest and memories. The thought of Lauro's delight in flying steadied her apprehensions, but she wrote, "If I die, I firmly believe it was meant." Overall, she had performed six solid week-long engagements plus a number of one- or three-night stands, for a total of sixty times.

Charis Cortese-de Bosis came to London. They had not met since the summer of 1930, and, as it was her first visit to London, Ruth took her about a great deal. From Paris, en route home to Rome, Charis wrote of her gratitude for so many lovely things: "Thank you for the tenderness with which you surrounded me in your lovely little house. I think we could not be fonder of each other than we are. I am so proud of my sister Ruth! I feel you as a continuation of [Lauro] in the deepest sense of the word, so much of him is still left in you, now and always. You carry on, Ruth, the flame of his life!" She signed herself "your sister Charis."

The year 1936 brought with it a tour of the six major Scandinavian cities, with fine press notices and quick, intelligent audiences. All the royals and diplomats turned out, she had tea at the palace, and her opening nights were gala affairs. Ruth thoroughly enjoyed this tour. "It makes all the difference, knowing people now in these countries." Then she performed in Brussels, The Hague, and Amsterdam, cities to which she would return many times.

During this London season, Ruth wrote: "The King [Edward VIII] has expressed a desire to hear me. I go on June 30 to Lady Cunard's. I would prefer *not* there, however felt I could not refuse." It was said that His Majesty became restless.

To Bill Carter, in Geneva, she wrote: "If not this year, we'll take a trip another year. That's the nice part about the Atlantic and the British Isles—they're so permanent and so, I feel, is my bank account. For which I thank God only—and the loyal public!"

In June, Amey Aldrich joined her brother, Chester Aldrich, now head of the American Academy in Rome, as his hostess. She brought messages to Lillian de Bosis from Ruth and, most importantly, copies of letters written to Ruth at the time of Lauro's flight and upon publication of his two books. For Signora de Bosis they were emotionally overwhelming. She responded to Ruth: "I must try to tell you a little about the rapture they have given me. . . . They are the confirmation of all that my heart desires. . . . 'Sorrow' is not the word—now and for some time I have left sorrow behind me and live in the presence of such unspeakable beauty and greatness. . . . I feel that you too have come to the same triumph of life over death. . . . So all is bright and clear between us and I need not try any longer to tell you nor to thank you for what you have done for him and so for me." Ruth wrote, "I feel as far beneath her as I did Lauro."

Ruth's London seasons were repeated nearly every year in June or July, and usually there were a number of tours in the United States and Canada. "Although at home I am always packing to go away!" Early in 1937, after an absence of twelve years, Ruth made a three-month tour across the northern states to San Francisco, to Honolulu for two performances at the university, a visit to the Dillinghams, returning through the Midwest—sixty-seven performances, nearly all one- or two-night stands. She grossed sixty-one thousand dollars. Then she took a long Islesboro summer holiday in expectation of her world tour.

Arriving in London late in November, Ruth gave a short Christmas season and spent the holidays with the Brand family at Eydon Hall. (Phyllis Brand, a sister of Nancy Astor, had died the previous January as the result of her overexertion in the hunting field.) Ruth went with them to Ditchley Park for the Astor family Christmas dinner with Nancy and Ronald Tree.

Mary Erdman, a new acquaintance, joined Ruth for this long tour. "An experiment, but I am pretty sure in my judgments of people." On New Year's Eve they sailed from Marseilles for Colombo, India, Malaysia, Australia, and New Zealand. Her "Great Journey" had begun. The insistent clamor for Ruth Draper's performances would keep her on tour for eight stimulating, rewarding but exhausting months.

A well-seasoned traveler, Ruth, prepared for all climates, carried six bags—including bags for her shawls and bits of costumes. For nearly seven weeks, she toured Ceylon (now Sri Lanka) and India. As guests of the viceroy in Delhi and the British governors in Madras, Bombay, and Calcutta, she reveled in the amenities and comforts of "Empire." On sight-seeing trips, in government rest houses or good hotels, she assuredly was under official auspices. She longed to meet more Indians and for Alice and Edward "to explain it all." It was some months before Ruth would say that the heat, the long, hot dirty journeys, and the bad theaters had been tiresome and that she would not again consider working in India. Without the comforts and amenities of "Empire," she might not have been able to carry out her schedule. Although dreading the heat, she "had made up [her] mind to enjoy it for I suppose I'll get nothing else," but it had been difficult.

On April 28, she wrote Ba, her half sister: "I got the impression that there is an increasing indifference and defeated feeling on the part of some of the British, as if they saw the writing on the wall—and as if the younger generation did not have the love and dedication and sense of 'service' that the old I.C.S. [Indian Civil Service] had. They come for the job and the salary and not to give themselves for the country's good as completely as the old ones did. I may be wrong."

On to Rangoon, Mandalay, and Bangkok, where Ruth, the indefatigable sight-seer, made a side trip to Angkor—"two days there, weird temple—stupendous—worth the long hot journey—eight hours by train and three by car." Then to

Penang, Kuala Lumpur, and Singapore. "Mary is ready to go home now. So am I, but my work has just begun. . . . Mary Erdman has been a very agreeable companion—not quite quick enough in seeing things and with no initiative but a good sport with charm and humor and tact. We've kept wonderfully well, though working in the heat is desperately hard."

From Singapore, Mary Erdman sailed for Hong Kong and Hawaii, and Ruth sailed for Java, Batavia, and Bali, which she found so enchanting, the people and life full of such grace and beauty that she would gladly have spent many more days there and flown to Australia. As a practical matter, however, she needed the ten-day quiet sea voyage to rest and to reorder her energies after the experiences of the past three months, so different in all respects from anything she had previously known.

The next four months became an unmitigated triumph. There had been nothing like it since Australia's own Dame Nellie Melba returned to tour after years of operatic acclaim in Europe and America. Expecting only dull people and average audiences, Ruth found warm, vigorous, healthy people and intelligent, quick audiences starved for the worlds she brought them. She extended her time and might easily have worked for another three or four months. Not by the "hundreds were people turned away" but by the thousands. It was exhilarating and rewarding, but a long, hard, demanding experience—every night and three matinees for two weeks in Sydney, nine performances a week for four weeks in Melbourne. Yet she enjoyed it all.

The vastness of the land, the hills, weekends at sheep stations, the baby lambs (an obsession), picnics overlooking miles and miles of rolling country and blue distant hills—she loved every minute of it. Dinner parties, supper parties, giving parties in return—all *great* fun!

Ruth scheduled four extra matinees just for school children, ages fourteen to seventeen; the matinees were attended by, it was estimated, seven thousand children. She wrote to Alice: "Never have I had such a responsive, quick and intelligent audience. It was amazing—so well behaved and adorable—beautiful young things—boys and girls. The children here are superb and it was so satisfying to realize how the teachers and parents responded. The place was sold out in a few hours, the schools buying great blocks of seats. The sound of that young laughter and swift applause rings in my ears and gives me new strength—for I'm rather tired—but it did me so much good!"

She found a new understanding of her gift. "I don't think I've ever had a more convincing sense that I was really giving delight and stimulating pleasure to so many people." On June 8, in a letter to Alice, Ruth said:

> I'm prolonging my stay—indeed it's next to impossible to leave. Never have I had such pressure, such acclaim, such obvious longing to have me go on. I could stay for months more! They are quite mad—they get in line at 5:30 a.m. to buy seats. Hundreds come 3 or 4 or 5 times.

Such silence, such concentrated attention and warm response. It's touching, so genuine, so direct and sincere. All kinds of people—rich, poor, doddering old, deaf, blind, eager young! I long to go home—it was a terrible sacrifice to stay even the three weeks more, but seemed foolish not to when I'm doing such unheard of business. I just thought hard of all the things I could do with the money and finally acquiesced.

At a conservative estimate, Ruth must have performed more than 130 times. In Australia alone, her manager estimated roughly, she was heard by over 120,000 people. Miss Draper's share of the box office in Australia was £18,323.6.9—the equivalent of approximately $50,000. "This will come in handy," she wrote to Dorothea, "for the less successful earners in the family in the years ahead."

Ruth Draper sailed for home on August 22, but there was one more performance en route: On the 25th the SS *Mariposa* called for several hours at Suva in the Fiji Islands. A matinee had been scheduled for the Suva Town Hall and promptly sold out—a month in advance. Ruth consented to a broadcast—which reached even to Tonga, sixteen hundred miles away, and it is told that in front of every shop in Suva that had a radio were gathered groups of Fijians, in their white lava lavas and fuzzy wuzzy hairdos, listening to Ruth Draper.

As this was a charity benefit, half the receipts went to the Suva Cottage House and half (£48.11.10) went to establish the Ruth Draper Benevolent Fund. The first beneficiary was an old Solomon Islander, in prison for life, to provide glasses to enable him to read—his one joy. They hoped Miss Draper would approve.

After a few months at home, Ruth sailed for Europe. It was 1939 and, with the war clouds gathering, Ruth's appreciation of London was heightened—its beauty, its associations, its friendships—heightened to a poignant, heartbreaking intensity. The preparations for war focused her apprehensions—yet London steadfastly appeared calm and secure. Paul Draper, her nephew, was dancing in London, his unique tap dancing to classical music. Rosa Lewis of the Cavendish Hotel in Jermyn Street—and Edwardian fame—went to see him. A week after her own opening, Ruth received a note from Rosa:

> We have been to see young Paul and think he is extremely clever. I want you to give a cocktail party here at my expense in memory of your brother whom nobody in the world has ever been like. So will you arrange a party here any time you wish.
>
> With love and affection from all your friends who were here last night and had been to the theatre. There is only one of everybody in the world.
>
> All my love, yours always gratefully,
>
> Edith and Rosa Lewis and all yours and Paul's friends

There is no evidence that Ruth accepted this offer. It seems unlikely.

Desperately anxious, Ruth returned to Paris for two weeks. "The dazzling beauty of it all went to my head like wine, I saw lots of lovely things and, though one is full of hope one cannot suppress a horrible fear that one may be looking at them for the last time. The danger seems to enhance the beauty and I felt like crying about five times a day."

"I am *torn* about coming home! I long for Islesboro but I am so happy here in many ways I don't want to ever come home! Save that I love you and want to see you again, and the many friends I love." And again to Alice, on the 23rd, she wrote: "General Herbert from whom I rent this house wired he had to return and would I please relinquish the house and go on Saturday. He is called up and must settle his affairs." So Ruth left the Cotswold house she had taken to be with the Vivantes and returned to London. "The King returns today to London and Parliament meets. Anything may happen in 24 hours." Ruth finally decided that it was wisest to return and on the 29th sailed in the French line's *Champlain*. On September 3, while her ship was still at sea, England and France were at war with Germany.

In January 1940, Ruth's war work began in earnest with a month-long cross-Canada tour for the Red Cross. After performing on the West Coast, she returned to New York to prepare for her South American tour.

Also aboard the SS *Uruguay* were Arthur Rubinstein, with his wife and children, and Professor and Mme. Henri Focillon. As the news from France became increasingly alarming, Ruth was grateful for Professor Focillon's calm historian's view of events. All the same, she was emotionally shattered and could barely contain her anger at the German stewards of the ship. She spent her evenings with the Focillons and Rubinsteins, and on tour their paths often crossed.

This three-month tour took Ruth the length of South America. She performed in Buenos Aires, Montevideo, Rosario, Cordoba, Santiago, Lima, and Quito. As usual, she found many delightful people, Victoria Ocampo being most congenial, and was feted by the American diplomats *en poste*. In all, she performed thirty-three times in nine cities, giving seven benefits for the Red Cross. She returned home by air on August 9 and went straight to Islesboro, where she began the first of six years of wartime summers devoted to caring for seven children (with three nannies) of English friends, sent (in 1941) to the States for safety. Not yet in their teens, they were all well mannered, well disciplined, "proper" English children who would never forget the fun they had and cherished the memory of their Islesboro summers. "Anxie" Gamble, who had been known as "the Irish angel" when she was nurse for Paul Draper's two sons in Edith Grove in London, was on hand to help out; Anxie had become a permanent fixture in the Draper families, beloved of them all, children and grown-ups alike. Justice Felix Frankfurter joined the adult circle, apparently enjoying it all, with Salvemini, Aileen Tone, Felix and Helen Salmond, and various friends and family members with their children. This pattern of gathering about her the many members of her family would continue each summer after the war. "I love having this old house full of young things, and I love feeding them and planning for their well-being."

In London, on October 1, 1941, Elena Vivante, Lauro's sister, broadcast to Italy in commemoration of Lauro's flight and death just ten years previously. She ended by saying:

> Happy is he that from the misery of everyday life can choose such a pure buoyant moment of liberty. A levity of spirit similar to the one that made the hearts of saints happy. My brother must have fallen in this supreme buoyancy of spirit—more fortunate than his companions who were stabbed by the fascists. Who could weep for him? His name lives in the hearts of the oppressed Italians, but remember him awaiting the day in which our country, vainly searching in the sombre cloud in which it lies, waits for it to rise up again. On that day there will be no Germans and no secret police, or non-secret police; and until that day, soul of my heart, comfort us while we wait.

It was Elena who understood Lauro's sacrifice.

During the years 1941–45, the years of the war, Ruth's life took on a different rhythm. She remained entirely within the United States and Canada, incessantly on the move, crisscrossing both countries nearly at random, performing almost exclusively to benefit the Red Cross and British War Relief, and for the entertainment of Canadian and American troops in army camps, air force bases, and hospitals. It was an enriching, exhausting experience, personally not remunerative. In no way did she spare herself. When home in New York, she worked at the Stage Door Canteen and had groups of sailors to supper in her apartment. She thought a good "home meal, comfortable chairs by the fireside, and a friendly welcome" would be the most supportive thing she could do for British boys so far from home. But she preferred being on the road as more worthwhile. Only over the Christmas holidays in 1942 did she have a season in New York, at the Little Theatre.

The touring was rigorous—bad hotels, not clean, and with deplorable food—but usually she could get a few supplies—milk, an egg, fruit, bread—and whip up her own meal. She had chance encounters that interested and stimulated her. Chatting with a train conductor, she outlined the plot of a new sketch that she was thinking about and was much amused when he said, "Gee! That would make a good movie!"

At this time of crisscrossing the country, Ruth Draper was on the eve of her sixtieth birthday. In one tour of sixty-two days, she gave forty-one performances in thirty-four towns. It is extraordinary, the equanimity with which she met the rigors of her long, uncertain, basically uncomfortable wartime tours. Only after three successive nights in sleepers, taken after her shows, did she write: "It will be thrilling to sleep in a bed tonight." But then she wrote: "I was called at 6:30 a.m. and we left at 6:45 after a cup of black coffee at the station lunch counter. It was dark but the tiny crescent [moon] and the dawn, so beautiful over the snow-covered hills and valleys that I was delighted to be up at that hour and wandering along in the filthy slow train." Of one seven-hour ride she wrote: "The dirtiest old car with straw seats, hitched to a freighter! Lunch at Howard Johnson's and a 60-mile motor drive, [then] a lovely bracing walk in the snow." Week after week it went on. For the most part, she chose to ignore the discomforts, savoring the warm human moments and holding them in her heart: "A warm and restful night on the train, delicious breakfast at a lunch counter with 50 aviators and sailors and a charming officer; a long day in my compartment, reading GBS [George Bernard Shaw], knitting and talking to three very interesting aviators. I believe I am at my best working and wandering."

In May 1943, Martha Draper, "Ba," the eldest sister, suffered a slight stroke. Just a year previously, after a visit to Ba, Ruth had written: "Barie, darling, how I loved being with you and I liked the quiet days best of all. How lovely to see so much of you with no sense of rush. Thank you for the lovely care and rest and sense of home that you give me—that I feel in your presence."

Ba died on June 29. A few days after the funeral, Ruth wrote to Alice: "I feel terribly sad—all beaten inside and the grim last moment was a shock—the fact that I didn't follow my impulse to open those doors [of the hearse] and ask them to put in the flowers is a bitter regret. One becomes so terrified of doing something impulsive with those strange men. Paul's flowers were buried with him—it was a kind of comfort. Ba's flowers seemed so to express her beauty and purity."

Professional bookings did not come readily to Ruth during these war years. Then managed by Sol Hurok, Ruth received the impression that he did not regard her as a really theatrical production. She frankly faced the reality that newer, younger, more glamorous performers of greater novelty were what the American public wanted. She engaged Harold Peat "to fill up a few weeks here and there. . . . I'll work where I can. I've rented my apartment to economize, so I'm footloose and free, which I like, but it's sad not to have any work." She hoped the Royal Canadian Air Force (RCAF) would want her in Canada for a tour of air force training camps. She would try to pick up jobs at bases in the United States. Actually, she was on the road a good part of the time. Her nephews John Carter and George Draper were at Fort Sill. John Carter wrote: "Aunt Ruth appeared in our mess hall at lunch time, dressed in a tweed suit, recited, wowed those present and then I drove her in a jeep around the Post! She was full of appreciative enthusiasm."

Ruth worried about all her friends in England, their husbands and sons. With Grace Martin she constantly sent off packages of food and warm clothing—hoping they would arrive—and arrive intact.

At last, in May 1945, England's war was over. The next few years were times of real austerity and hardship. The winter of 1946–47 was bone chilling and doubled the hardships. But in May of 1946, Ruth was able to return—with apprehension, deep humility, and near overwhelming emotion.

8

The Drapers after World War II

"WE WERE A LARGE, ACTIVE AND LOVING FAMILY," said Dorothea, "and Ruth was the one who shone—just why, I don't know."

There must have been—there were—tensions. Ruth's success and fame had been so immediate, apparently so effortless, and so very visible. Yet each one accomplished good things and, in diverse ways, made a difference to many people.

Although the Carters were based in New York after 1922, Edward's work took him, with *Alice*, around the world about every two years. Alice wrote long interesting letters from the Orient and from the Trans-Siberian Railway as she journeyed alone with her young daughter from Shanghai to Moscow. They were much in Russia at this period, where Alice, immersed in work for people, saw things more tolerantly than did Ruth in 1929. During the Second World War, both Carters were involved in relief work, Edward heading up the Russian War Relief and Alice as president of the China Aid Council. Until his death in 1954, Edward pursued his Asian concerns in United Nations economic commissions and other educational organizations. Alice was active, when in New York, with Play Schools, the YWCA, the Harlem Hospital School of Nursing, and the League of Women Voters. In 1969 she was cited as "Woman of the Year" by the National Council of Women.

On Alice's seventy-fifth birthday, Mrs. Franklin D. Roosevelt wrote her a letter that, perhaps, sums up her years: "I have the deepest admiration for the way you have lived your life and the things you have achieved. You have never been afraid to live and that is one of the most important things that can happen to any of us." Of the eight Draper children, it was Alice who lived most deeply among the realities and the peoples of the world.

Charles had become one of the original partners of H. N. Whitney and Sons, and continued so when it merged with W. H. Goadby and Company. He became president of the Association of Stock Exchange Firms. He remained a bachelor until he was fifty-seven, when he married Jean McGinley Moore, a delightful and charming widow with three grown children. Her sister-in-law called her "a great girl."

Charles was amused and proud of Ruth's accomplishments and called her, fondly, "the prima donna." Ruth depended upon him and when, in 1947, he would die of a heart attack, she wrote: "He was a wonderful brother and head of our happy family. . . . He was so happy and so well and to die in his sleep was a perfect end for him."

A young cousin wrote: "Characters like Charles—so wholly fitted for living—with serenity and uprightness and tolerance and kindness and warm tenderness for those he loved—and ready wisdom—why are there not more like him in this sorry world. . . . His lines were all straight and true and good." As a friend remarked, "Difficult as Dorothea could be, she married two of the nicest men in New York!"

Widowed by the death of Linzee Blagden in 1936, *Dorothea* in 1938 married Henry James III, nephew of Henry James the novelist and son of William James the psychologist and philosopher. Everyone was delighted. The family had known him for years and Ruth wrote, "I think Harry has been in love with [Doro] for a long time." At the end of her life, Dorothea said, "Those were *happy* years." As a friend remarked, "Difficult as Dorothea could be, she married two of the nicest men in New York!"

Harry James was a delightful, rather pedantic, crisp, and humorous man. He graduated from Harvard and took his law degree there in 1904. He had a long career in executive positions at the highest level with the Rockefeller Institute for Medical Research and, from 1934 until his too-early death in 1947, as chairman of the board of the Teachers Insurance and Annuity Association. He served twelve years as an overseer of Harvard University and was a fellow from 1936 to 1947. He was meticulous, precise, and methodical, and his broad experience made him an effective trustee for four large and prestigious educational institutions. He edited the letters of his father, William James, in 1920 and in 1930 received a Pulitzer prize for his biography of Charles W. Eliot, the great president of Harvard.

Dorothea, too, was concerned about people, about excellence, about making a difference. She was a leader in the drive to establish the Columbia-Presbyterian Medical Center, president of the board of managers of the Bellevue Hospital School of Nursing, and president of the Colony Club (a long-established women's club in New York). Appropriately, this was Dorothea's club; Ruth belonged to the Cosmopolitan Club, which was newer and less formal.

Because of her long service to medical education, New York University honored Dorothea in 1945 with a degree of doctor of humane letters. Already Ruth had received two honorary degrees and Dorothea, with her many years of constructive work, found this disconcerting. Dorothea's degree somewhat relieved the tension that had grown up between them, for Dorothea was jealous; she was jealous of Ruth's fame and, particularly, of Ruth's dazzling host of friends in England and in Europe. Basically kind and warmhearted, she held many devoted friends of her own; but those were snobbish times, and Dorothea was very much of her time.

There were passages of real asperity between them, often sparked by Dorothea's jealousy: Bridling at Ruth's reference to a trip to Vienna in 1956 to "work," Dorothea snorted, "What kind of 'work' do you do?"

"I do monologues, in case you don't remember." Ruth might well have said, "I earn my living by monologues."

Later, Dorothea remarked, "Ruth was very rude to me, today." Dorothea had worked, and worked very hard indeed, but she perhaps defined it differently: she led, she presided, she saw to it that things were accomplished.

Even so, Dorothea remained truly devoted to Ruth, and together they formed a unit of help for anyone in the family in need of moral support or of financial and practical assistance. They were solidly united, too, in their efforts to do the right thing, as they saw the right thing, for their nephews and nieces. They looked with a sharp eye on any family newcomers, and it must have been a daunting experience to marry into the Draper clan, aside from the sheer force of personalities. When Bill Carter presented his recently wed wife, "G. G.," to Aunt Doro in the summer of 1956, she was greeted with, "Well, thank God *Ruth* likes you!"

After Ruth's death, Dorothea would say to this caller: "My life is both dimmed and lighted by constant thought of her. But, oh, the hurt of going on without her!" In her last years, Dorothea still minced no words, but she could be almost mellow, warmer, rather lonely, and very, very funny.

George had gone to Zurich for two years following his divorce; he studied there with Jung and was himself psychoanalyzed. He then pursued his convictions in constitutional medicine and wrote *Human Constitution* and many other remarkable books in this field, particularly as it related to cardiac diseases and to polio, in which he was a specialist. It was because of his recognized authority that he had immediately been called in when Franklin D. Roosevelt contracted polio in 1921. Having known Roosevelt at Groton and Harvard, George was particularly sensitive to FDR's psychological needs; he gave Eleanor Roosevelt significant support in her decisive fight to return FDR to an active life of political purpose. At Campobello, and for many months after, while Franklin was "suffering the tortures of the damned," George had been impressed by his courage and his will to get well, a will that never faltered. Such was his sensitivity and understanding that in later years, when FDR was in the White House, George refrained from calling on him lest Franklin be reminded of his suffering.

With insight and intuition, a farseeing genius, George projected the known far into the unknown, but he was a generation too soon and received little comprehension or support from his colleagues—the historic fate of pioneers. In later years, however, doctors whom he had taught as young students would send word to him that medical science was at last accepting much that he had taught them years before. It was George who came nearest to being the scholar son that his mother had longed for.

Several years after his divorce, George Draper met Elisabeth Carrington Frank, recently divorced from Seth Low. She was perceptive and understanding, with a distinctive wit and humor. That George was twenty years older made no difference; they were married in 1935. With a son of her own, she became a supportive, sympathetic stepmother. Elisabeth Draper was an established decorator of quiet, private spaces—of homes and of the executive offices and meeting rooms of banks and corporations.

In World War II, George applied his scientific methods of constitutional medicine in evaluating the fitness of military aircraft pilots for combat service.

Ruth and George had a devoted, unusually companionable relationship. She addressed him as "Geog"—pronounced "jog." She agonized over his frustrations and disappointments, for he was ambitious and worked desperately hard to prove his ideas. He was doing valuable work. Alice and Dorothea were well aware that George felt acutely Ruth's early and easy success, a tension of which she remained totally unaware; it never would have occurred to Ruth that there could be any sense of rivalry. In time, he took real pride in her life and career. In degree of talent and intuition, he was the one most similar to her.

When, in 1950, George would begin his long ordeal with Parkinson's Disease, Ruth would be deeply concerned, thoughtful, tactful, and generous, appreciative and supportive of her sister-in-law. Emotionally, she was shattered, appalled by the suffering that he bore with great courage, reading by the hour from two books that throughout his life he kept by him—the Bible and Shakespeare—holding that in them was all truth and wisdom. In many places, he crossed out the word *love* and substituted *wisdom*.

Long concerned with public education, *Martha* had been a founder in 1895 of the Public Education Association, serving as its president for a number of years and as a member of the board of education from 1910–17. Later she was appointed to the Friedsam Commission, whose findings led to new principles of state aid to education and in teachers' salaries. In 1933, Governor Lehman would appoint her to the Commission on the Cost of Public Education. For forty-eight years, with knowledge and effectiveness, Martha would serve public education in New York City.

Martha was seventy-nine when she died in 1943. *The New York Times* ran an editorial under the heading "A Distinguished New Yorker." It read: "Her poise, kindliness and dignity marked her unmistakably a lady of the old school. . . . With her death New York City loses another of those splendid women who dealt selflessly and energetically and intelligently with the City's unique problems. . . . Hers was a good fruitful life." "Barie," said a younger cousin, "was one of our chief blessings."

Ruth Dana Draper's sister, *Eunice Dana*, was so prominent a figure in the lives of the Draper children that her presence should be recorded. "Aunt Nin," gallant and dauntless, was an active and militant pioneer from the early days in the women's suffrage leadership—the Woman's Political Union—and as a champion of women's rights. For picketing the White House, she was arrested with twenty-five others in 1917, tried, and sent to a federal workhouse. Near collapse from their shocking treatment there, she was released on parole. But she remained militantly active in the National Woman's Party. It was said that she was one of the greatest money raisers for the suffrage movement.

In 1935, George Draper called on his aunt in her apartment across the hall from Ruth, at 66 East 79th Street. She was eighty-one. He found her sitting, as always, upright and alert in a straight-backed chair, in the sun, by the window of her living room: tall spare frame, her long thin face strong and her glance keen, her gray hair swept up into a knot on top of her head. "How are you, Aunt Nin—and what are you reading?"

"I'm pretty well, thank you George, although I don't see very well. But you know, George, it's a funny thing, whenever I read anything about sex, I see perfectly."

"Spicey," Elisabeth Draper called her. Aunt Nin did not like Lauro and considered Ruth to be living in sin.

9

Family and Friends

RUTH DRAPER'S FOCAL POINT WAS HER WORK, the compelling force of her life, to which it gave coherence. She had no interest in "causes"; she did not actively help those in need but gave benefits, personal checks. To her friends she gave concern, appreciation, love, and material, practical aid. In a special category were Lauro's anti-Fascist colleagues or their widows and children, to whom she gave friendship and constant thought for their well-being, as well as practical aid.

It must clearly be understood, however, that this was not anti-Fascist activism in any sense of the word. It was her compassionate concern for their sacrifices to Lauro's cause and her sense of his responsibility to them. "It is what he would wish to do." Most strongly, it was a way of not letting go of Lauro. Each one she touched kept alive her tie to him; each one confirmed her role in his life.

How much did her family understand and appreciate Ruth's way of life? Each one must have had a particular view of so complex a sister and varying reactions to her fame. Only Alice seems to have brought a matter-of-fact acceptance, but perhaps she had a different point of view, for she considered the person, not the fame. In March 1937 from Honolulu, where their paths crossed for several days, Alice wrote to Dorothea:

> Ruth has had a great success and I have been asked regularly if I do not feel proud of her. Of course I answer appropriately. But somehow I feel I should feel more excitement in my pride. Do you feel pride in what she does in her performances? Somehow I am much prouder of all that she does by her thoughtfulness and concern and her sincerity and independence. She is really such a grand person. I often wonder what she will do when she no longer can command this constant adulation. It will be a great test of her character.

From a reading of her letters, it is clear that Ruth looked to Alice for an understanding of her life in all its nuances—its heights and its depths—and a sympathetic understanding of her emotional response, sensitive, imaginative, and highly sentimental as she was. It was Alice, as one of her nieces said, who "knew what went on in the trenches."

True to their upbringing and their kind hearts, Ruth and Dorothea had constant concern for their nieces and nephews—for their well-being and the quality of their lives—and were regarded, in consequence, as interfering, even meddlesome and not minding their own business. Yet it *was* their business; it was the *family*, and they could not condone independence of behavior that disregarded the *standards* of the Draper family, disregarded its *pride*, disregarded its innate discipline and *dignity*, or disregarded its position in society.

In the first generation of Draper-Dana children—Ruth and Dorothea's generation—the standard was consciously maintained. Although Ruth broke away to the theatre, she did so on her own terms and remained within the family's social framework. Although Alice's life was quite different in its purpose and experience, she in no manner diminished its united image. Only Paul was a disturbance—but he had an addiction, and in his lifetime, its treatment was not recognized.

But the next generation—the nieces and nephews and their children—was a *different* generation, full of individuals determined to live their own lives in their own way in a very different world. There was no longer the same responsibility to family stability. This was a great anxiety and sadness to Ruth and Dorothea, those two pillars of dignity and propriety and rectitude. Dorothea was the more pragmatic and could deal with situations with wit and humor. Ruth was dogmatic and deadly serious. But love was at the root of it all, and this was understood by their friends. Ann Holmes wrote to Alice: "I remember how you told about it all when you were young—and I thought how lovely to have sisters and to like them as you all liked each other. I think that is a great thing that the Draper girls have given to the world—your great family affection."

In the telling of Ruth Draper, the positive so greatly outweighs the negative as to strain credulity—but that is the preponderance of evidence. The evidence, so far as her work is concerned, is well documented: To read through her albums of press notices, and of letters, becomes, after the first twenty minutes or so, a bit of a bore, the praise is so fulsome, so steady, and the bemused amazement so consistent. The negative notices were, perhaps, half a dozen and were confined to a German critic and a Swedish critic who possibly did not understand and American critics who fretted only that she had nothing new.

In her personal relationships, the lack of negatives also is striking. Not everyone loved Ruth Draper, but almost everyone admired her genius. Her special qualities largely outshone her faults, and her sparkling, devoted friendship was a treasure to be cherished. Beyond doubt she was a unique personality, demanding and difficult as she often could be.

The history, the art, the beauty in Europe were so important in Ruth's life that she was determined her nieces and nephews should have some experience of Europe. It was not her knowledge she wished to share but her enthusiasm. In her own youth, in trips with her mother, Ruth had been told what to see—"Don't look at that, look at this"—and she could think only of doing the same for the next generation. She would expose them to the beauties of Italy and Paris and expect an appreciative if not emotional response. Never, it seems, did it occur to her that this was another generation, differently educated, and that her young people might have a slightly broader view of what would nourish their growth, a less directed sense of beauty and experience. Even so, it was all to the good.

In many ways, Ruth was exactly like her own mother, certain that she knew best and commanding the interest and activity of the young minds that were, by that count, two generations on. Exactly what this writer met, in my twenties, from my great aunts, who were of Mrs. Draper's generation; there was no possibility of compromise, for that generation bred an indomitable force of character. This was not an intellectual determination; they simply *knew* what was right.

In 1927, Ruth and Dorothea took Alice Carter's eighteen-year-old twin sons on a routine sight-seeing in Italy. They were amused but receptive, and it made a strong link with the aunts. In 1935, Barbara Longcope, a young cousin, and Diana, George Draper's daughter, slightly older, were given a trip. In London, every moment was planned, and, Barbara said, Ruth "commanded" their interest with "frightening force"; of Diana she asked a level of cultural awareness beyond her capacity. In 1954, Anne Draper, Smudge Draper's daughter, Ruth's grand-niece, flew over to join Aunt Ruth in London. Now twenty and very shy, she looked forward to sharing a little of Ruth's London life, of her theater backstage, simply to be with her aunt in *her* world. But Ruth had arranged for the sons and daughters of her own friends to take Anne to lunches and dinners, parties and weekend events, to "see that she had a good time." Not happy, for Anne, but redeemed later by Paris and Italy, Villa Solaia and Berenson at I Tatti. "Short, but I think it was better than nothing," said Ruth, satisfied that she had done the right thing. So she had, but it never occurred to her to ask any of these nice young people what might interest them and to build on their strengths. Child that she herself was, Ruth seemed oblivious to their sensibilities.

She met her match, however, in Bill Carter's newly wed wife—Dutch and French—fortified by the realities of long years under German-Nazi occupation, by effectively obtaining the release of her mother from German incarceration. Visiting Aunt Ruth in 1956, with Bill, G. G. wished to shop for a good British tweed coat. Ruth wanted her to "go about London to see beautiful buildings"; but G. G. had lived her forty-some years with Europe's beautiful buildings and was determined to have her coat—which she was happily still wearing thirty years later. Frustrated and baffled, Ruth wrote to Dorothea, "At least, why couldn't she get something lovely for the evening?" This would, probably, have been quite inappropriate to the social life of two hard-working, modestly paid UNESCO staff in postwar Paris.

How does one reconcile this contradiction between Ruth's stage creations— so true to human nature—and her apparent incomprehension of changed lives and attitudes in a new generation and a different social milieu? It may come down simply to two separate intellectual processes and the fact that Ruth never quite made the adjustment to changing conditions within the Draper family. With all her pioneering independence, Ruth remained firmly within the pattern of her mother's generation.

Young John Carter came off more easily. Upon his graduation from college, Ruth gave him a thousand dollars to take a trip on his own. As his parents were then in China, Ruth and Dorothea, always supportive, attended his graduation ceremonies.

Those nieces and nephews who "hated Auntie's guts" did so because she asked too much of them—more curiosity, more interest, more appreciation than they had to give. She could be bossy and demanding, but it was all for the best. And, as Alice said, the next generation gave her an opportunity to express her love and concern and generosity. She agonized over their faults and disappointments and gloried in their successes. Probably they never understood how deeply she loved them. But she was, after all, the daughter of an imperious mother and an all-knowing imperious generation. The adjustments did not come easily, if at all. Charles was forever making peace in the family—where Ruth was regarded, surely, more as a relative than as a genius.

Although compassion and sensitivity to people were an integral part of her genius, Ruth could, nevertheless, subject people to inexcusable disregard—even humiliation—inflicting social wounds that would leave scars on the heart and memory. Forgetfulness or impatience could in no way excuse her lack of consideration—especially for some who might feel at a disadvantage with her. These extraordinary lapses often took place within her extended family, wherein she undoubtedly felt in a position of authority and direction. Perhaps all in-laws were, to her, basically intruders—the Drapers were such a self-consciously cohesive clan. And yet, she could meet people at all levels with warmth and compassion, even with love. It was a blind spot greatly to be wondered at and impossible to defend.

Ruth was a combination of the whimsical, impetuous enthusiast—the child—savoring each moment as if unrelated to the whole, and the strong-minded, disciplined performer. Those who served her did so willingly and dealt cheerfully with her temperament as they found it; they recognized her special qualities and felt privileged in their roles. Perhaps they understood her the best, not expecting her to be like themselves.

At Dark Harbor, Islesboro, in the big house that her mother had built in 1897, Ruth had her own tightly controlled world. She loved to gather family and friends about her and all their young children, as well as the seven English children (with three nannies), who had been sent to America for safety during the war by their parents, Ruth's friends. One of the adult guests visiting in those years, seemingly enjoying the variety of ages, was Justice Felix Frankfurter. Salvemini also was a regular guest. Other adults came and went: Aileen Tone, Helen and Felix Salmond, the Bolaffios, with Anxie, "the Irish angel," an indispensable friend to them all.

The children later spoke of how it was: Ruth had well-tried resources to keep the children busy—for amusement, for learning, for fun in a family group, for *discipline*. Sitting at the table for meals, her young nieces endured a three-foot yardstick down their backs—for posture. There were few toys, but a collection—

an accumulation—of games: chess, Scrabble, Monopoly, cards, checkers, crayons and clay, and, for dressing up, a big trunk in the attic with a variety of wonderful clothes—everyone dressed up. On her travels, Ruth bought a great many postcards, many of the same subject, scenes, architecture, paintings, and sculpture that she thought important or beautiful, and these she kept in a drawer of the desk in her small writing room near the front door. Whenever a child wished to write a friend or family, Ruth would say: "You wish to write your little friend? Well, just choose a card, or more, and write on the back. I will get stamps and we'll send them off."

While the elders took naps, Ruth would gather the small-fry around her on a big deeply cushioned couch in a shady corner of the porch and read to them, weeping, too, over *The Wind in the Willows* and *Charlotte's Web*, entering completely into their world. She recited poetry to them and they to her, and so they knew how important a place it held in her life. She offered a penny for each line of poetry they memorized, and two cents for each line of Shakespeare—"28 cents for a Sonnet, this was riches!" They walked in the woods to gather small plants and ferns and moss to make miniature gardens, and Ruth told stories of the things around them, and tales of the elves there, and of "Charlotte," the spider for whom they caught flies and whose web was washed away in a storm. Each child had his or her own room, as Ruth held this to be important. She went every night to tuck each one in, with a special story or poem. It was an ordered, routine life, each hour planned—no idle moments.

Childhood is resilient, and they loved the life at Islesboro, sharing the outdoors, the woods and the beach with her, but living up to Auntie's standards may not always have been easy. The small English children, during the war, were "proper" English children, disciplined and under control of their nannies, accustomed to toeing a strict line of good behavior. But for children brought up less formally, sometimes there were difficulties. Anne Holmes said, "It was hard work, staying with Ruth—living up to her standard!" It was as though Ruth had her own concept of "children"; she could be ecstatic about children, watching them at play by the hour. But it was her idealized image of CHILD, rather than the actual child, that she held in her mind, and all children, particularly family children, were expected to conform. When she gave them her attention, it was total, participating concentration—telling terrifying witch stories with them in her bed, in her arms, "this wonderful woman who could send us to the moon" but who would then switch off—"Time to go to bed, now!" And, next morning, she would be busy with her own concerns, disengaged, distanced, officious. They would be confused and hurt, wondering what they had done to displease her. "Where has she gone, that wonderful woman, who filled our imaginations?" Did her role-playing extend so far? Yet the children of Sylvia Weld, in Boston, *her* childhood's friend, eagerly looked forward to Ruth's visits: "We were in and out of her room and went with her to the theatre to 'maid' the great actress. We *loved* her visits—they were happy and exciting." Yet, while children loved her and anticipated her visits with pleasure, her greeting often overwhelmed them with its enthusiasm and emphasis: "Oh, you *darling* children, I am so glad to see you, you don't *know* how I have *longed* to see you!"

Anne Draper was seven years old in 1943 when her father, Smudge Draper, crashed his disabled RAF plane into a field to avoid crashing into a school full of children. Smudge and Anne's mother, Marcia Tucker, had divorced, and she shortly remarried. Dark Harbor, with Aunt Ruth, was Anne's refuge, bringing stability; and it was Anxie who could talk with her about her father—Anxie had cared for him as a baby. It was Anxie who took this very shy child into her arms, who listened and explained. Anxie was patient and reasonable and common-sense and knew how to deal with Anne's temperament and temper tantrums, how to deal with her growing pains. Aunt Ruth seemed not to be capable of this sort of nurturing and understanding. With all her own emotionalism, she simply walked away from Anne's. The subtleties of discipline were, apparently, beyond her.

It is interesting to note that in later years, when Anne expressed a wish to go on the stage, Ruth called down upon her, in the most scathing terms, all the prejudice and determination of immorality prevalent in her own youth, which she had calmly ignored in 1920 and which by the 1950s was largely mitigated. Art had overcome scandal. Even so, Ruth carefully maintained her own position: She was in the theatre but not "of the theatre." Uniquely, she was author, director, producer, and performer of her own work and so controlled her own professional environment, where she made all the decisions. But her "precious little Anne, so very like me," going "on the stage" in the usual way, triggered all of her inherited inhibitions.

The household equanimity that Ruth engendered at Islesboro was quite remarkable, the children and grown-ups entirely at ease and comfortable with each other, this group of varied ages, temperaments, and nationalities. Each child had his or her own place. There were boundaries, recognized but livable. It made for unusual peace and harmony and enjoyment. Ruth was a FORCE, sometimes intimidating to the young—even to the not so young—trying to meet the high standard she demanded, but even in their very young years she was an influence—by the very force of her character and personality—by her strength. It did them no harm and surely much good, for even today, Aunt Ruth's standards have left their mark.

"I guess its lucky I had no children," she wrote to Dorothea in 1934. "Their imperfections would have hurt me so—and my disappointment would have hurt them so."

Ruth brought her own personal world to the house on Islesboro and took little or no part in the goings-on of the summer families. She knew them all and had many great friends among those households, but she did not play golf or bridge, did not "dine" back and forth. The local people, however, were another matter; she knew them all, their ramifications, their stories and personalities. In many ways, they were closest to her. She went to church and each summer gave a benefit performance. Islesboro was her refuge, and in it she found peace and refreshment; here was *her* world, and she controlled it.

A cherished member of this summer group was Gaetano Salvemini, Lauro's friend, who had been with Ruth in Paris at the time of his disappearance and remained her staunch friend and "loving old uncle"; devoted to him, she wished to do what she could to ease his years of exile. Widely regarded as one of the great men of his time, he nevertheless lived a very straightened life. This is his story:

Of peasant stock from Molfetta in the Apulia—his grandfather was a fisherman—Salvemini escaped the limitations of his southern homeland by attending school in Florence and obtaining a scholarship to the university there. With a brilliant mind, great determination, and a countryman's strength, in spite of very meager resources, he became a historian and teacher of history who steadfastly sought truth in all his activities.

Salvemini was a big lumbering man with a peasant's gait and a Pugliese accent. He had a snub nose, a handsome head, bald and Socratic, and great humor with a hearty irresistible laugh. Mary and Bernard Berenson became his close friends. His honesty, natural goodness, and great kindness and compassion opened many doors.

At twenty-four, Salvemini married his Maria from Molfetta, and they had five children. He wrote, "In my family life I am so happy that I am frightened." He was teaching and living in Messina at the time of the earthquake in 1908. His family, asleep at the time, were wiped out. Salvemini himself dropped five stories with the outside wall, but, miraculously, was saved. He never really got over his grief nor the hope that his youngest, the three-year old Ughetto, would be found.

After this blow, Salvemini resumed his lectures at the University of Florence and immersed himself in politics. Long a Socialist, he became associated with the Rosselli brothers and with them, in 1911, started the political newspaper *L'Unita*.

After serving in the army as a volunteer in the 1914–18 war, Salvemini was elected to Parliament with a large majority, but in the changing political climate, he decided not to run for a second term in 1922. Increasingly and vocally opposed to Fascism, he soon was in trouble with the Regime. Because of his association, again, with the Rosselli brothers, this time in the anti-Fascist journal *Non Mollare* (Stand Fast), he thought Florence too dangerous a place for him and moved to Rome, where shortly, in June 1925, he was arrested.

After thirty-six weeks in prison in Rome, Salvemini was tried— the Fascists provoking a riot—and was found neither guilty nor acquitted but was granted provisional liberty—he would be accompanied by two guards. The Socialist deputy, Matteotti, had been murdered the year before, others had been brutally beaten or murdered for similar activities, and Salvemini well knew that his own time was running out. He spent several weeks traveling about Italy to annoy and confuse his guards; finally he was able to slip away from them, and, by zigzagging across northern Italy, constantly changing trains, he arrived near the frontier. Guided by a former student, he crossed on foot, through a pass in the Alps, at night.

For some years Salvemini had spent his summer holiday in England to learn the language, quite rightly foreseeing that he would become a refugee. Now, in England, he found kindness and hospitality, going first to the home of Bertrand Russell, whose wife, Alys, was the sister of Mary Berenson. He was welcomed by the anti-Fascist exiles and also among the English intellectuals, by Isabelle Massey, who translated his lectures and articles from Italian into English, and by Marion Enthoven (later Rawson); they became his friends, his typists and translators—he could not, he said, have survived without them. In time, they became Ruth's friends and admirers also.

Soon Salvemini resigned his professorship at the university. Professors in Italy were told to take an oath in support of the regime—"Academic freedom has been suppressed, without which there is no dignity left in the teaching of history as I understand it," he said. Then he added that he would return "when we have got a civilized government again." After his straightforward remarks in a lecture at the National Liberal Club in London, the Fascist government took away his citizenship. So, at the age of fifty-two, Salvemini began a new life, in a different country, with a different language. He called himself neither "exile" nor "refugee" but *fuoruschito*—one whose exile is a deliberate choice.

As Lauro began his work with the Italy-America Society, Salvemini also was in the United States to deliver a series of lectures. In 1929, again in Paris, with Carlo Rosselli and Emilio Lussu, Salvemini organized *Giustizia e Liberta* (Justice and Liberty); it became the focal point for efforts by the anti-Fascists of the left. Not a political party, not advocating violence, it called for personal and political freedom. Recent friends, Salvemini the Socialist and Lauro the Monarchist (or so he appeared to be) could not agree, but in their hatred of Fascism and love of democratic freedom, they were united. Salvemini, however, never believed that Fascism would succumb quickly to an internal crisis.

On the recommendation of Professor George La Piana of Harvard, Salvemini was invited in 1930 to teach there for four months at a fee of four thousand dollars ("One year of life," he said). Yale invited him to teach for five months in 1932–33 at a fee of five thousand dollars.

For some time Ruth had been searching for a more enduring memorial to Lauro, other than his books. She discussed her ideas with Gilbert Murray at Oxford, with George La Piana at Harvard, and with Salvemini, about whose financial situation she was greatly concerned. She decided to propose to Harvard the establishment, in the Department of History, of *The Lauro de Bosis Lectureship in the History of Italian Civilization*; early in December 1933, Harvard College accepted Ruth's offer to found a series of six lectures and a seminar during the second half of the academic year. The yearly fee proposed was two thousand dollars, and Harvard was pleased to accept her recommendation of Gaetano Salvemini for the first appointment. The commitment was for one year and would be continued on a yearly basis for five years. The donor wished to remain anonymous.

When the formal, public announcement was made, the representative in Boston of the Fascist government promptly protested through a member of the faculty "who seems to have assumed the task of serving the Fascist interests at Harvard." But neither the President, Dr. James B. Conant, nor the Dean paid attention to the protest, and President Conant's response was an invitation to Salvemini to dine.

Salvemini was meticulously careful to express none of his political opinions. He was prepared to give his lectures in scholarly fashion, to be accepted as a scholar and not as a politician, and, at the end of his sixth lecture, to thank the unknown donor and then to "explain who de Bosis was and why his name is to be recorded."

This appointment was a lifesaver for Salvemini. He would live in Leverett House, and while financially limited, intellectually he was rich beyond his dreams with the seemingly inexhaustible resources of the Widener Library available to him.

This is the man who, from this time on, would spend part of each summer at Dark Harbor, where he became an established member of Ruth's extended family. Admired and highly regarded by his fellow guests, dearly loved by all the children in those evening pastimes he joined with hearty enthusiasm and shouts of laughter, he was surrounded by friends. In February 1936, writing to thank Ruth for some introductions she had arranged for him, he said, "Everything I am doing, all the happiness I am enjoying, despite these bad times, I owe to you, dear, dear Ruth."

In May 1939, Ruth sent fifty thousand dollars to Harvard to endow the Lauro de Bosis Lectureship as a half-year course. Largely motivated by her wish to sustain Salvemini in his exile, she nevertheless wrote Harvard: "I wish to endow the Lectureship in [the memory of Lauro de Bosis] that the story of his determination, courage and idealism may serve as an inspiration and example to young persons, and that at the same time they may profit by studies in the history of Italian Civilization." She wished "Italian Civilization" to be interpreted in the broadest sense, and it was her "hope that the lectures in this course will illuminate the gifts which Italian culture has given to the world." She hoped, also, that the lecturers would "be men of Liberal conviction."

"Ruth," said Isabelle Massey to Neville Rogers, "was an architect of Friendship. . . . Never can a personality of such forcefulness have been more universally beloved." And Laura Chanler White said to this writer, "I never heard anyone make a catty remark about Ruth." Civilized and humane, Ruth Draper looked upon each person in simple human terms, not in terms of whatever position they might hold of influence or power or rank. Her friends were of all ages and nationalities, of varied social levels, of diverse interests and associations, each one evaluated in her mind as a *person*.

With another war beginning, she was, in 1939, most consciously aware of her friends. Those in England, now in such physical danger and with husbands and sons in the fighting forces, were constantly in her anxious thoughts. Concerned and apprehensive, she felt keenly the limitations of her ability to help: She was *here*, and they were *there*; there was little she could do other than lend moral support and, practically, send parcels of food and other necessities—which might or might not arrive intact, or at all. Concern for her older friends was particularly poignant and real. *If* they survived the air raids, would they still survive the hardships and deprivations of wartime? Would she see them again? In fact, almost all of them would come through.

These older friends—men and women—were cherished by Ruth as irreplaceable treasure; she held their memories and experiences to provide almost an extension of her own life. While she gave a great deal to them in the way of attention, appreciation—indeed of love—she also received affection and appreciation in return. It may be worth telling, briefly, of what experience Ruth found in these lives to nourish her, for she eagerly sought their tales of earlier times.

Louisa, Lady Antrim, Countess to the eleventh Earl, was born in 1855, third daughter to General the Hon. Charles Gray, private secretary to Prince Albert, the Prince Consort, and, after his death, secretary to the Queen. Lady Antrim became Lady in Waiting to Queen Victoria and served for various periods from 1890 to 1901—the old Queen's final eleven years—and then as Lady in Waiting to Queen Alexandra until 1910. Lady Antrim was, herself, a fine and upright figure who carried out her royal duties with competence, humor, great tact, and calmness. She knew all the rules. She accompanied Queen Victoria to her winter holidays in the south of France and was in Waiting at the Royal functions: the Queen's state visits to Berlin and to Ireland and the Kaiser's state visit to London. Over a period of twenty years, she was in service to the two Queens, becoming, as Queen Victoria put it, "almost one of ourselves." At ninety-one, when doing some sketching, she said, "I never painted until I was 80, but I've done a great deal since."

The Mudie sisters were, for Ruth, like Lady Antrim, a window to the past. They, of their own experience, knew the heroes of the Risorgimento, Mazzini, and those about him, who were familiars in the Mudie home. They had been intimately associated with the de Bosis family and the life of Rome, where for fifty winters their friends had been almost exclusively Italian—"We never knew the English in Rome after those far-off days when the Trollopes lived there and Margaret Oliphant." Mary Mudie, born in 1847, well remembered being taken at the age of four by her father to St. Paul's Cathedral immediately after Wellington's funeral in November 1852 to view his tomb, covered by flowers and flags. She spoke from her own observation of Queen Victoria's Jubilee and that of George V. When George V died, she thought back to the mourning in the streets for Wellington, for Prince Albert, for Queen Victoria, and for Edward VII. "This," she said, "was *far* more general, *far* more personal, *deeper*." Ruth was exceptionally devoted to the Mudies not only for themselves but also for their close link to Lauro. When in London, she kept their rooms filled with flowers, sent Fred with the Rolls to take them for drives, and provided innumerable and varied gifts for their comfort and pleasure. She took her nephew, Bill Carter, to meet them. "They were," he said, "perky, talky, *good* tea!"

Mrs. Yates Thompson, her mother's close friend, became a close and supportive friend to Ruth. Her much older husband (born 1838) had been Head Boy at Harrow when Palmerston was Prime Minister and, at one time, proprietor of the *Pall Mall Gazette*; he was a barrister and a bibliographer who made a notable collection of illuminated manuscripts—always no more than one hundred of the finest examples he could acquire. Mrs. Draper wrote of him, "He is a scholar, a millionaire and a man of experience; he is opinionated, sharp and British."

Mrs. Thompson was the elder daughter of George Smith, founder of the *Dictionary of National Biography*, a publisher and friend to Thackery (on whose knee his daughter sat as a child), Charlotte Brontë, Darwin, Ruskin, Browning, and Trollope. From her country home at Oving, Mrs. Thompson provided Ruth with vegetables, fruit, flowers, and butter and cream from her fine herd of Jerseys. In later years, crippled with arthritis, she oversaw her large estate from a battery-powered bath chair.

Ruth often visited Oving, as well as 19 Portman Square—a great house of Victorian ease and culture, where the telephone was banned and from which—as from Oving—Mrs. Thompson drove forth in her carriage drawn by a fine pair of horses. She was a famous hostess, serving the best of food and wine (her superb sherry had been sent round the world in her father's ships). She spanned the generations in her informed and witty conversation, and her guests were a challenge to her great qualities.

In 1935, Ruth wrote to Mrs. Thompson: "You mean so much of my love for England and I don't feel it's quite all here until I see you." Ruth held Mrs. Thompson at the top of her list of great old ladies whose active minds, great wit, and long memories contributed so much to her pleasure in England and to whom she was so cherished a friend.

Eliza Wedgwood, great-great-granddaughter of Josiah Wedgwood, founder of the Wedgwood potteries, was long a beneficent resident of Stanton, in the Cotswolds. She was, to Ruth, "the finest person I know, a pure delight, with the vitality of youth—with such laughter and wisdom and pity and tolerance and wit all merged—to be with her is like drinking some rich cordial that gives one new life." Eliza was seventy-five when Ruth wrote this of her to Dorothea in 1934. Sitting by her window, always open so that she might feed any hungry bird and with the front door—painted Mediterranean blue by her friend John Singer Sargent—always open to any of the village people who might need her help, Eliza was definitely a "character"—gregarious, garrulous, loving and disliking with equal enthusiasm, plain and not in the least fashionable, she was the treasured friend of everyone in the village. When the spire of the Stanton church was urgently in need of repair, Ruth gave a benefit performance; she loved this Cotswold village, with its single street and sixteenth- and seventeenth-century houses.

Eliza was friend to all the household at Stanway, home of the Charteris family for four hundred years. About a mile distant from Stanton, Stanway itself was unique. The home of Lord Elcho, who succeeded his father, the tenth Earl Wemyss, of whom Matthew Arnold said, "The cock of his Lordship's hat is one of the finest and most aristocratic things we have." Lord Elcho had held that title for so many years that even after he succeeded his father in 1914, his wife continued to be known as Mary Elcho. She was one of the beautiful Wyndham sisters, whose portrait by Sargent now hangs in the Metropolitan Museum in New York. Stanway itself, built of golden Cotswold stone—comfortable, shabby—was and still is a beloved and beautiful house, full of laughing guests and good talk. Mary Elcho was at the core of The Souls, that late 1880s–1890s group of young, intelligent, witty, and cultivated men and women who set an intellectual standard for the forty or fifty members of their social group. Against this background, Ruth, through Eliza, came to know the household, particularly two of the daughters, Mary Strickland and Cynthia Asquith, who for nineteen years was secretary and friend to James M. Barrie. Such were the wheels within wheels of Ruth's friendships.

In Canada she had old Miss Wilks at Cruickston Park, Galt, Ontario. Ruth wrote to Martha in 1943: "It's just like stepping into a Victorian novel. The old portraits seem alive—the stuffed furniture sat in by lively ghosts—the million nicknacks just touched by loving hands. It is stuffed with romance, tradition, humor and charm, and I revel in its atmosphere. Miss Wilks is vigorous and full of fun and her memory is fabulous—I am so amused by my ability to follow her recollections of people. . . . I delight in this extraordinary vitalizing of the past, through her vivid personality, and the fantastic number and interest of objects." "Imagination and memories," said Ruth, "what gifts from the Gods!"

There were some, however, whom Ruth did not cherish: for one, Elizabeth Robins (then in her ninetieth year), an American actress largely responsible for introducing Ibsen to the English stage, who lived with Octavia Wilberforce—doctor to Virginia Woolf—near Brighton. Ruth writes of "unwanted and burdensome affection" and refers to Elizabeth Robins as "the old tyrant." Obviously, they asked more of Ruth than she was prepared to give.

Besides her elderly women, Ruth had her cherished "old boys": Henry James, Bernard Berenson, Sir James M. Barrie, and Gilbert Murray, born 1866, the great Greek scholar and professor at Oxford who wrote a preface to her translation of Lauro's *Icaro* and advised her in its publication.

Sir Sydney Cockerall, born 1867, was a bookman all his life. He had been secretary to William Morris at the Kelmscott Press and became his literary executor, as well as literary executor for Thomas Hardy and Wilfred Scawen Blunt. For nearly thirty years, he was director of the Fitzwilliam Museum in Cambridge.

In New York, Ruth had "CCB," Charles Culp Burlingham—born in 1858, he remembered Lincoln's lying in state. He was a brilliant admiralty lawyer who regarded Ruth almost as a daughter. Often, in the evening after dinner, she would drop in for a chat. He was close to Salvemini and Bolaffio, and would be desolate at her sudden death.

These "elders" were a wonderful, special category of friends who provided another dimension to Ruth's life. The strong backbone of friendship, however, lay in her contemporaries, the friends of her youth and, particularly, of her childhood. In England, of course, she had the whole Phipps family: Dame Jessie (Mrs. William Walton Phipps), who became a member of the London County Council, her son, Paul Phipps, whom Ruth regarded almost as a brother and who married Nora, youngest sister of Nancy Langhorne Astor. Another sister, Phyllis, married the distinguished banker, Robert Brand (later Baron Brand of Eydon), who was extensively involved in South African affairs with Lord Milner and, since then, in international economic affairs. Nancy Astor and the life at Cliveden were a part of Ruth's growing up, though Nancy, "the soul of indiscretion," and her unpredictable behavior rather discomforted her.

It is significant that nearly all her older friends were English—there was no comparable group at home. This relates, perhaps, to her happiness, her sense of congeniality in England—indeed in Europe—and to her lifelong and apparently compelling need for the richer, deeper culture of these older countries. It was more than just the fact of Empire; it was the space and depth of history, of tradition, of association, the assurance brought by generations of participation—the security of establishment. It may well, too, have freed her from her Puritan background.

No matter how many stars there were in her constellation, it was the childhood friends at home who were the core of the tried, dependable, enduring group of whom Ruth said: "There's nothing like an old friendship like ours, it seems so secure and different from other friendships." Included were friends like Mercer Howe, Sylvia Weld, Alice Boit Burnham—"people one loves and feels cosy with—dear faithful old friends"—Malvina Hoffman, now an accomplished sculptor, and Corinne Robinson Alsop, niece of Theodore Roosevelt, who served with her husband in the Connecticut legislature for many years, a very strong woman, intellectual and active in civic affairs, whom Ruth held in some awe.

Aileen Tone, Harriet Marple, and Helen Salmond (wife of the cellist Felix Salmond) came a little later. They, to Ruth's grand-niece, Anne Draper, seemed "a band of special women; without the usual housewifely interests, theirs was a bond of different concerns, a bond of varied experience and, above all, a strong spiritual bond." All these friends at home seemed to a young cousin "Although chronologically old [they] were so youthful in spirit that one never thought they might end."

For a woman so strong, so dominating, yet so reserved and basically so humble, Ruth established an amazing range of friendships, not only the well tried friends of her youth—all much of a kind—but also the mix of acquaintances of her days "on the road," friendships that ripened into something less casual. Of these, let it be said, that however much they simply were attracted to the "star," those who "ripened" did so because there was a foundation of rapport, interest, and mutual appreciation.

What was her quality that attracted so many and such a variety of enduring relationships? Vital and laughing, Ruth was fundamentally kind, she cared, she respected individuality, she did not intrude and she listened—her interest held by the differences. Constitutionally naive and in no way an intellectual, Ruth attracted a diversity of highly intellectual, highly educated, widely experienced people—Learned Hand, Maynard Keynes, Geoffrey Keynes, Air Chief Marshall Sir William Elliott, Isaiah Berlin, Barbara Ward, and all her "old boys" noted above—men and women who held her friendship and their meetings as real treasure. Perhaps it was, as Alice Burnham wrote, that "Ruth brought beauty and laughter and warmth into one's life in a way that was all her own; her emotions were so intense—whether acting or just living—you were always part of them," and to Aileen Tone, that "she gave of herself in such a wonderful way."

10

Harvest Years

Courage, enthusiasm, awareness, if only one can keep these to the end.
—Ruth Draper, February 13, 1937

THE 1930S WERE THE YEARS OF COURAGE—even to 1946. The early years of the next decade were driven by Ruth's enthusiasm—and determination. Her "work" was the mainspring of her life, and she could not—would not—contemplate her life without it.

The war in Europe was over, and her English audiences wanted her back. The year 1946 was one like no other; with humility, awe, and apprehension, she began to pick up the old relationships. On February 28, she sailed, with two thousand others, in the *RMS Queen Elizabeth*, so long and so lately a troopship. Launched just as the war began, its trial run being a secret, silent dash across the Atlantic to New York Harbor, this magnificent ship was then outfitted only to carry thousands of troops. Now, after five years of sailing to all parts of the globe, she was worn and shabby and smelly, and comfort was totally lacking. It epitomized all that Ruth knew and all that she expected to find in the war-torn world abroad. Her emotions were at a high level of intensity.

"Fred and the Rolls" awaited her boat train at Waterloo, and she could "barely restrain [her] impulse to kiss him!" Lorna Carew had reserved her suite at the Hyde Park Hotel, overlooking Kensington Gardens and the Serpentine. The rooms were full of flowers; messages and letters lay on the desk. The telephone rang—she was back in London.

The welcome from her friends—and from her audiences—was beyond her belief—she, who had been fed and warm for six years and not in danger of bombs, was humbled before them, yet they greeted her warmly—in the theatre with an ovation. She went about London, weeping at the destruction, humbled by "the way I am remembered."

Immediately, Ruth went to Hornchurch with flowers for Smudge Draper's grave and learned from the headmaster how Smudge did not eject from his crippled plane, loaded with fuel and ammunition, but controlled it to crash in an empty field, giving his own life to save that of nearly a thousand children in the school building. She met Sheila Connolly, a student, who tended the plants at his grave and who held the Sanders Draper Scholarship. In due time, Ruth would become godmother to Sheila's first child.

Queen Mary came to a matinee, bringing Princess Elizabeth, and the Queen came, bringing Princess Margaret Rose. Ruth broadcast, over BBC on March 16, a moving, heartfelt message: "The gift of my talent . . . seems a small return for the great gifts of the spirit which I, and countless thousands throughout the world have received from you during the past six-and-a-half years." With "pride and with most true affection," she thanked the British people for their kindnesses to the Americans who had been in England during the war. From this, letters poured in, touching letters, each one to be acknowledged.

At the end of her London season (four performances a week for three weeks), Ruth was tired from the emotion and excitement and apprehensive about the tour ahead—sixteen consecutive weeks in sixteen cities, under possibly difficult conditions. Austerity was not over, nor would it be for another five or more years, and in many ways was tighter than during the war.

Her new sketch, *Vive la France—1940*, which dramatized the spirit of Resistance in France, was a triumph. Ruth's British public loved too all the well-worn characters who grew a little over the years as they themselves had grown. She had become a legend, and her houses were sold out. She throve on it all and wrote, "I'm never better or happier than when I'm working—inwardly happy and content." She gave 126 shows—to, probably, 252,000 people—talking onstage, she estimated, for 315 hours.

To the lord mayor of each city visited she sent a check for relief work, in "heartfelt gratitude for the overwhelming welcome that has been given me and my imaginary company." And to her stage manager, Harley Merica, a check for a hundred pounds in thanks for their "happy association" on this British tour.

Just as she began her tour, Ruth received a real blow—news of the death of Ned Sheldon. Only fourteen months younger, he had been an unfailing resource of encouragement, advice, and support in her life. A brilliant young playwright, he had been stricken in 1921 with a progressive arthritis; within a few years he became rigidly immobilized and, finally, totally blind. Of great strength of personality, tremendous charm, and extraordinary memory, he was visited by an ever-widening circle of friends as he lay on his bed, always neatly shaved, dressed in collar, tie, and jacket, with his hands hidden under the blue coverlet. After his blindness, there was a black band across his eyes. To his cheerful penthouse room at 35 East 84th Street, filled with flowers, books, and photographs, came theatre people, writers, musicians, men and women in the forefront of their lives, to discuss their work, to receive his advice and wisdom. Always they left with their lives strengthened and their problems clarified. He could talk with strangers as though he had known them all their lives, seemingly with uncanny powers of perception and understanding. Anne Lindbergh said, "One went away refreshed and stimulated." His dinner guests were served delicious, well-chosen meals, while he lay unmoving yet fully participating as host. News of the world was read to him, and he was well informed of all that went on in the theater. Playwrights and actors came for his wisdom, and, as Ruth wrote, "It was like going to Heaven and talking to God in a cosy way." In writing to Alice she now said: "I can't grasp it, he was such a symbol of immortality in his life that I somehow never thought of life without him. His spirit always was, and always will be like a radiant arrow of direction and triumph." It was Ned who said: "When Ruth Draper performs, a Holy Ghost descends upon her shoulder." Ned's approval of her work—which she always performed for him, standing on a table, when he could still see but no longer turn his head—was the ultimate accolade. Many felt that his sensitivity of mind and appreciation seemed to be increased rather than lessened by his isolation.

Now, at last, Ruth could return to Italy—after sixteen long, anxious years. First to Siena for two weeks at Villa Solaia, the old house on its hill, and the Vivante family—only recently returned from their seven-year exile in wartime England. "Caramadre" was there—their first meeting since the summer of 1930. In Florence, Ruth renewed her friendship with her Italian friends: B. B. at Vallombrosa, and with Reggie Temple—long a fixture in the expatriate English colony—who, after 1931, had carried Ruth's letters to and from Vittorio and the de Bosis family.

Ruth's meeting with Mario Vinciguerra and his daughter, Claudina, now twenty-two, must have been almost unbearably poignant. As Lauro's anti-Fascist colleague, he had been arrested, brutally beaten, and jailed for mailing Lauro's letters during his absence in New York—an absence that Lauro came bitterly to regret and that changed the course of his life. Ruth would keep in touch with Vinciguerra and Claudina, with the widows of Renzo Rendi, arrested at the same time, and Carlo Rosselli, and their children, sending the occasional generous check. Bitter as was her hatred of Fascism, it was compassion that prompted her and the knowledge of Lauro's sense of obligation, which she felt in duty bound to honor.

Returning to Paris for two weeks, Ruth gave four shows. Lugné-Poe had died in 1940, but she was fortunate to find an associate of Reinhardt, who had managed her in Berlin and Vienna in 1928, to manage her in Paris at the *Comedie des Champs-Elysees*. Comfortably visiting Anne and Dean Jay in their Avenue Foch apartment, Ruth "walked [her] feet off" to renew her vision of Paris, untouched and more than ever beautiful after five years of German occupation. A trip with Eva Dahlgren to the invasion beaches and villages on the invasion route was heartbreaking, horrible, moving, and revealing, but it enabled her to envision the scene. "I feel I must grasp that tragedy and glory and heroic vision."

The next year, back in London, Ruth was well looked after by her British friends and as ever active.

> The telephone rings every few minutes; a box of apples has just arrived, two grouse are hanging outside the window, brought to me last night! I have eggs from the Highlands, butter from Bedfordshire, honey from Edinburgh and jam from Manchester friends. Life is bursting and the days fly. Yesterday I started at 10:30, after dictating for an hour and

a half, stopped to get two bags I was having fixed for Gretchen [Green]; went to the Theatre and posed until 12:30 to have my pictures taken on the stage; delightful lunch party at the Connaught and sat next Harold Nicolson's son—a brilliant, charming young man. . . . Then I went to look at a Chinese bronze I've bought, then to sit with Elena [Rathbone?] and have a lovely talk, and then to say goodbye to Johnny and Anne [Holmes]; then to tea with Elsie and a nice talk, then to my Theatre where I gave a particularly good performance; then to a supper party. Bed at 12:30. Some non-stop day! Generally I try to get home for tea and a slight rest—at least pause and silence—for an hour before my show!

She wrote Alice:

I'm so sorry I've few days left, my heart is sad at leaving. Life is so complete, so full, so vivid and adorable. There is so much beauty one forgets the ugliness, so much warmth one forgets the cold, so much love one forgets the hate in the world. Life is too rich and wonderful. My, how I hate to leave all this here—it seems so stupid to stop, but I've always had to face the same choice, and it gets harder each time with the awful thought that there must be a last time sometime! It's all going full swing and it's terribly hard to end it—to break it all off by the deliberate action of getting on a ship and sailing away— yet I know I'm coming back to more love and warmth and the thrill of your welcome!

On December 7, she sailed in the *Queen Elizabeth*.

I have so many I love at home and my sweet flat awaiting me, full of memories, of comfort, and bits of beauty gleaned from my rich life of wandering and work. So I'm drawn back, but already dream of my return to Europe.

In London, early in November 1948, Queen Mary, as she so often did, attended one of Ruth's matinees. The birth of Princess Elizabeth's first child was shortly expected so the Queen had a telephone rigged into her box at the theatre so that she could be informed immediately. Prince Charles did not arrive until November 14.

A pattern of activity now became clearly established: tours in the United States and Canada, a London season almost every year, often a fall season, Dublin in 1950 and 1953, occasional engagements on the Continent—Scandinavia, Holland, frequently Paris, every year to Italy to see Lauro's mother until her death in 1952, to see Salvemini. There were visits to Villa Solaia and to the old tower, Portonovo, the children eagerly welcoming her visits—"she brought such lovely presents"—and then often hiding because Ruth was determined to arrange picnics and excursions—go here, go there, see this, see that. She thought everyone should be active, every opportunity to see and do must be seized—"beautiful places, beautiful and interesting things." In Italy she gave many charity benefits, sometimes donating her entire proceeds.

And *every* summer: two or three months at Dark Harbor, with the old house full of children, family in and out, tired friends. She rejoiced to give them a rest, good meals, and laughter—always laughter.

Nieces and nephews remained her concern. She tried not to interfere—rarely was she at home long enough to do very much. But in 1951, when Bill Carter joined her in London, she wrote his mother to announce, with some satisfaction, that she had bought him a "splendid winter coat at Burberry's, got his boots to Fortnum and Mason's for repairs and now I'm working on his hat!"

Every year across the Atlantic by ship, often two round-trips, until 1954 when she took to the air. She had enjoyed the more leisurely, sometimes more interesting, crossings—as in the SS *Queen Mary* over the 1952 New Year, with Winston Churchill, again prime minister, and a party of thirty en route to confer with President Truman. She had many friends in the group and saw much of them.

There were serious concerns too, which baffled and shocked her. Ruth's nephew, Paul Draper, had perfected a unique talent for tap dancing to classical music. With Larry Adler, the harmonica virtuoso, he had had eight very successful years dancing nationwide in concert tours. Then he and Adler were accused, in a letter published by a Hearst newspaper columnist, of being Communists. These were the searing years of the House Committee on Un-American Activities and the attorney general's list. They were years also when war with Soviet Russia seemed a clear possibility, a dreadful time of political fear with anti-Communist hysteria warping reason and judgment.

In an attempt to clear their names, Draper and Adler jointly brought suit for libel against the writer of the letter, Mrs. Hester McCullough of Greenwich, Connecticut. Although left-wing liberals, they firmly denied being members of the Communist Party. The trial ended in a hung jury, but it effectively ended the professional careers of both men in the United States.

Ruth was totally unable to comprehend the causes—and the effects—of the situation, except that disaster was implicit—"How *could* this happen?" "Ruth," said Salvemini, "has no understanding of politics." She could grasp only that "Paul was young and unwise."

However, Ruth stood by Paul with all the moral and practical support she could muster. With his family he came to London in December 1950 hoping to find work there or on the Continent. Aunt Ruth remained in London "to give them a happy Christmas." She had taken a house at 37 Chapel Street, and Paul would be right next door. On tour in Stockholm, she sent Lorna Carew a check for twenty pounds and a long list of staples and fresh foods to put in the house for their arrival.

Eventually, Ruth realized that the only way to give Paul a start was to share the bill with him in London, and when, later, he returned to New York, she appeared with him on Broadway and on short tours. Dorothea said, "Ruth has a tender concern for that little family," and together they faced the realities of his situation and did a great deal to ease their straightened life.

Conditions on tour were difficult still, and in Ireland her usual milk and biscuits after her evening show was not enough; now it was cheese and biscuits and Guiness' Stout. "The stages are like ice boxes with strong winds blowing. Don't know how I survive."

In June of 1951, Ruth "opened" a barge anchored in the Thames near Windsor (which, it was said, she had bought to be used for charity events). Thinking of her own Lady of the Manor of her sketch *Opening a Bazaar*, she said, "It was too ridiculous—I felt just like myself!"

In the autumn of 1950, from the Hassler in Rome, Ruth wrote of her very social visit:

> More benefits, Lauro's mother and family whom I run in to see every day. Luncheons, cocktails, teas, dinner every day—a strange, amusing, exciting life with political friends—men who have been in prison— friends of Salvemini and Lauro, mixed with worldly people, many of whom I really despise, but who have heavenly houses and food and are very kind and amusing to see as part of this bewildering city of history and beauty and tragedy and flowers and memories and thrills of the mighty past all mixed up!

Ruth had a long talk with Maria Rosselli, the widow of Carlo Rosselli. In the midst of his spectacular and active work as an anti-Fascist, Carlo was murdered, with his brother Nello, in France on July 13, 1937. It was Carlo, with three others, who escaped *confino* on the Island of Lipari in 1929, in a dangerous conspiracy. This year, the graves of the Rosselli brothers, in a moving ceremony, were transferred to the Trespiano Cemetery in Florence, where they lie in a special quadrangle surrounded by cypress trees. In due time, Salvemini would join his colleagues there. Off the Corso are now a small Piazza Salvemini and the viale Fratelli Rosselli.

This, too, was a year of honors for Ruth. King George VI awarded her the Order of the British Empire, Hon. Commander (CBE). As a special honor, he himself wished to present her with the insignia at Buckingham Palace. Ruth was, of course, deeply appreciative. Then the University of Edinburgh wished to honor her with the doctor of laws degree. "I'd rather have Edinburgh's tribute than any in the world! It is sporting of them! An honorary degree to an actor!"

This was Ruth's fourth honorary degree: Hamilton College in 1924 (master of arts), their first such honor to a woman, University of Maine in 1941 (doctor of fine arts), and Smith College in 1947 (doctor of humanities). In 1954 would come her fifth such honor, from Cambridge University (doctor of laws), where she had many friends. Ruth would stay with the Master of Trinity College, G. M. Trevelyan, and his wife. The Vice Master, Harry Hollond, the active executive of the college, would give a luncheon for her in his rooms on Nevile's Court. These rooms, originally, were the rooms of Thomas Nevile, who had had the building erected around 1612, while he was Master. The guests, some of the great men then at Trinity, were delighted to meet her so simply.

In 1941 she had written: "It is all very impressive but I can't help laughing inside for the last thing I am is a scholar and a cap with a golden tassel and velvet-trimmed gown are symbols of high mental achievement, not a touch of a fairy's wand at birth."

However, her honors were leveled off in Boston, when she met an old friend on the steps of the Chilton Club.

"Hello, Ruth, still at it?"

"Yes."

"Good for you—but you'll never be as good as your mother was!"

In 1951 Ruth was sixty-six years old. She had planned to retire when she was fifty, but she seemed unable to stop. She was having too much fun, all doors were open to her, and London held all the personal and cultural treasure she could dream of. And Italy held treasure, too, but of a different magnitude. She created no new characters. She was too busy, and her life was too full, too rich, too engrossing to allow the climate and focus, the years of interior thought, that she needed to build new characters and the world and people around them.

These were the years of Ruth's increasing awareness of her own mortality. There were constant allusions: "I've not much time left!" "I must see—must see—must see—in case one can't come again." She seemed her usual self, full of gaiety and youth and spirit—but how long could she keep it up? "My wonderful life goes miraculously on!" she said and set out on tour again. She knew it was wonderful, she knew it was a miracle, and it was all such fun. She was not old in her appearance in character on stage—her voice, expressions, gestures, and movements were as young as she wished them to be. But she had become very deaf and had a heart problem and always carried nitroglycerine tablets in a small silver pillbox. Only Alice knew this, and her dresser, Wilhelima Reavis. She knew time was running out and seemed determine to live and work to the limit—until her force was spent. She could not face a long decline with clipped wings.

George Draper had now developed Parkinson's Disease. This was shattering to Ruth who wrote: "My tragic brother lives on, alas, his mind more and more clouded, his body still strong, tho' useless. How cruel these long deaths are! It's so sad to see him I can hardly bear it!" This, to Ruth, was an unnerving experience, and when she went to see George, she could deal with it only by denying her usual way with him—bringing a rice pudding or other offering she had made, she did so with elaborate chatter, almost baby talk. She simply could not face the situation. She did not stay long.

With this tragedy before her, she accepted the quick death of Edward Carter, following a stroke, with an understanding she might otherwise not have had.

The year 1954 began with a three-week run at the Bijou Theatre with Paul Draper. She no longer went uptown to her apartment between the matinee and evening performances but took a hotel room nearby to rest. Then she played a week each, alone, in Boston and Washington, where she visited the house where

Lincoln died: "I was terribly moved—a deep emotion gives one a curious lift and a moral cleansing. What a tragedy that was—and remains—like the Crucifixion— a source of *true* emotion, and the sordid little boarding house rooms, such a frame for the picture they evoke! I should like to have knelt down."

The year 1956 would become a compact review—almost a reliving—of Ruth Draper's years of work and wandering; it was a microcosm of the last thirty-six years—half her life—the life that she chose and built for herself—the life that enchanted her friends and puzzled her family. In this, her 72nd year, Ruth Draper seemed to reach out to the whole of her life, to touch again all that she had most cared for over the long years of her triumphs and tours, all that she could not let go of—every place, each person, remembering each emotion, the fun, the sorrows, the happiness, the excitement, and, above all, the beauty she cherished.

A careful reading of her letters leaves the clear impression that Ruth was fully aware that her time was running out and was determined to savor to the full every last look and last visit to all the places and people who meant most to her. In the meantime, the show must go on.

After a few joint appearances with Paul, Ruth Draper began the year as she had begun her career—with a month of one-night stands on the college and high school circuit, managed by Harold R. Peat. She sometimes wondered why she persisted, with no new material to offer and costs so high as to make the effort hardly worthwhile. Forty years ago RUTH DRAPER had been new and fresh and costs appropriate. Some loyalty drove her—though she had, perhaps, been around too long—and entertainment, something new, seemed more to the public taste in the United States.

This year the seasoned traveler had found even the prospect of planning the trip abroad to be daunting. But she carried it off—force of habit, perhaps. Now, from Vienna, from Ireland, from London she wrote voluminous letters to Alice about summer plans at Islesboro: Eleven beds—but was there enough bed linen? She fussed about who would come and on what dates; she listed the staples to be ordered—milk, groceries, coal, wood—and advised Alice where to place the orders and a word about each person to be dealt with. Alice, capable and experienced, had been managing households around the world for more than forty years, but there was no item Ruth failed to write about in exhaustive detail, letter after letter, week after week. Then she worried about Alice and all the work and decisions this put upon her. Never before, over the years, had she been so consumed, so fussed.

However, they all turned up, friends and family, children and parents, and everything went smoothly. It was a happy summer. She went about the island to chat with her old friends, all the Islesboro families she had known since childhood, many of whom were closer than her summer neighbors. She gave her annual benefit for the church. Quietly Ruth touched again all points of contact with her youth, with sixty years of deep happiness and memories. This year Ruth did not join the scramble to the beach, saying only that she "felt odd, in the early mornings"; she did not swim so often in the icy water; she decided to sell her little sail-boat, as she no longer had the strength to handle it alone. And in telling her niece Penelope of this, while sailing gently across the harbor on a brilliantly clear "blue" day, she added, in a most curious tone of voice, "Isn't it a shame that one has to die and leave all this."

However, the "call of the road" could not be resisted, and Ruth was here and there all fall—Oklahoma to Boston. Apparently her ageless, vital self, she attended the bridal dinner and the wedding of Eva Rubinstein; Arthur Rubinstein could speak only of her youth, her joy, and her genius.

Ruth did not give her usual Christmas party and opened on Christmas night for a four-week season at the Plymouth Theatre in New York. The day before she had told her dentist that she was so tired she did not know how she could perform. Each evening that week she scheduled the same program: *A Children's Party, In a Railway Station on the Western Plains, Three Women and Mr. Clifford, A Scottish Immigrant at Ellis Island*. On Wednesday and Saturday there also were matinees; she dreaded the two performances. The opening went well, and Ruth hoped to over-come her fatigue with the stimulation of enthusiastic audiences full of young people.

At the mid-week matinee, Ruth told Gerald O'Brien, her stage manager, that she was dropping the *Railway Station*—too exhausting—and would do the *Art Exhibition* instead. At the Saturday matinee, she mixed the sequence of happen-ings in this sketch, evoked some entirely new characters, and new incidents were brought in. The sketch ran four minutes longer than the usual fifteen minutes, and when she came off, Ruth said to Gerald O'Brien: "I just went blank and kept on talking. I never did that before." Obviously, she was disturbed.

That Saturday night, the 29th, in her last character, Lesley MacGregor, the Highland lass at Ellis Island come to marry her young man after three year's sepa-ration, finally sees him in a crowd and rushes off, stage right, her face radiant, eager, certain of happiness, calling out, "Sandy, my Sandy—I'm here!"

The ovation was long; the packed house standing to cheer and applaud a su-perb performance. She was content. She asked to be driven to see the Christmas lights and, arriving home, ate her supper and went to bed. At 11:30 the next morn-ing, her maid found her—apparently sleeping quietly. She had died peacefully a few hours before.

Paul came at once, and Ruthie Carter, and Alice as soon as she returned from church; Doro came, and Harriet and Aileen. Ruth's doctor came. Her electrocar-diogram had shown no change over the last ten years; her energy and walking had been that of a woman twenty years younger, but heart accidents were unpredict-able. Doro said: "I think she just spent herself beyond her endurance. Her cour-age sped her on just too swiftly. But she couldn't have borne the restraint and pain of illness." And Alice said, "She could not have lived without her work." That was the great—the only—consolation. Ruth had gone suddenly, without any fuss, in dignity and privacy, as she had lived. But her death, so totally unexpected, within hours of coming offstage, was a stunning blow to her family and friends as well as to her vast audience around the world. In London, when word came, the audience at the St. James stood with bowed heads in a minute of silence. The great lights over the marquee of the Playhouse Theatre in New York, read simply, RUTH DRAPER, and remained up, unlit, until after her funeral.

The dramatic critic, Philip Hope-Wallace, in the *London Time and Tide*, January, 5, 1957, summed up her meaning for them all:

> Alas for the loss of Ruth Draper, for we lose with her a mirror of the world, with all its human and social foibles which had delighted us for a long generation. She will become a legend; we shall tell the rising generations of her magic, awkwardly trying to imitate and pass on to them the characters she created for us and failing dismally to convey what she alone could convey.
>
> We shall not look upon her like again. Her success as an artist came as much from the depth and generosity of her character as from her precision in observing and skill in recapturing the essence of so many different characters. Underlying the laughter, there was always compassion. We shall miss her, not only as a unique personality of the twentieth century stage, not only as an entertainer who made us laugh and gave us the rare delight of watching a supreme technical artist, but one who, when all was over, made us like our neighbors better and enjoy the world more.

As announced in the *Court Circular*, a memorial service (organized by Joyce Grenfell with Anne Holmes and John Phipps) was held in London on January 10 at St. Martin's in the Fields, Trafalgar Square. Thelma Cazalet-Keir arranged the white and yellow flowers, with pots of poinsettia; the Christmas tree, fully lit, remained up. Acting as ushers were Lord Salter, Air Chief Marshall Sir William Elliot, The Hon. James Smith, John C. Phipps, Hamish Hamilton, and Reginald P. Grenfell (husband of Joyce). The vicar, the Reverend Austen Williams, read the Anglican service. There was a choir of eight mixed voices, and some of the same music as used in New York was played. Lord Brand read the 1st Lesson—Solomon III:1–9—and John Phipps the 2nd Lesson—I Corinthians XV:50–58. There were a number of special prayers, but one, written by Joyce Grenfell with the vicar, particularly should be remembered:

> O Heavenly Father, from whom cometh every good and perfect gift, we thank Thee for the delight and joy Thy servant Ruth shared with so many; for her unending generosity and untiring help to those in need; for all her life and art; grant that we, with a like loyalty in friendship and devotion in work may spend our talents in the service of others, and so serve the best and the highest we know that we, with her, may help to build Thy kingdom; through Jesus Christ our Lord. Amen.

Bill Carter, with G. G., came from Paris to represent the Draper family and sat in the front pew with Joyce Grenfell, Anne Holmes, John Phipps, and Captain and Mrs. William D. Phipps. After the service, Anne Holmes gave a family luncheon in her house on Carlyle Square. All Ruth's English and Scottish friends turned out for her—the list in the *Times* named over a hundred. The American ambassador was represented by Harriet Aldrich, her old friend, and the English stage by Dame Edith Evans, Irene Worth, and Ernest Thesiger; Cecil Madden represented BBC-TV. The Mudie sisters' niece, Mrs. Trenchard Cox, was there, and Harley Merica, Fred, her chauffeur, Marion Rawson, Neville Rogers, and Lorna Carew. The Gaters, of course, and the Stanleys, the Countess of Antrim, Baroness Ravensdale, Lady Fermoy, all came, with "theatre servants" and staff from houses in which she had played, and taxi drivers who never missed seeing her. The church was crammed. "The Vicar did the Service quite beautifully," wrote Joyce Grenfell to Alice and Dorothea. "He has a magnificent and rich voice and a great sense of occasion. Affection was the keynote, together with triumph." But Anne Holmes wrote, privately, to Alice that she "would have liked a little sentiment, somehow, and a little warmth. Ruth's eyes filled with tears so easily when she was stirred or moved, and that side of it all got left out." But it was a dignified, triumphant, and "proper" service, in the English tradition, and Ruth would have liked that.

Grace Church in New York on January 2 was packed for Ruth's funeral. Her nephews, Paul Draper and John Carter, Joyce Grenfell's brother Thomas Phipps, and Ruth's managers, Charles Bowden and Richard Barr, with her stage manager, Gerald O'Brien, were the six ushers.

The rector read the Episcopal service, and in the chancel, Lillian and Carol Fuchs played Mozart on unaccompanied viola and violin; at the end, the organ played the Bach Passacaglia in C Minor as Ruth was borne head high slowly down the aisle, her worn shawls crowned by white roses, deeply draping the casket. Alice and Dorothea walked close behind, followed by the next generations of the Draper family with the friends of a lifetime, Corinne Alsop, Aileen Tone, Malvina Hoffman, Harriet Marple, her social world as well as the world of the theatre.

In June, at Dark Harbor, Alice with her daughter Ruthie, rowed out into Gilkey's Harbor, near 700-Acre Island, and, as Ruth wished, scattered her ashes, with flowers, over the waters she had so loved and upon which she had spent the most peaceful and happy hours of her life.

Dorothea said: "The compass of the light Ruth shed is incredible. She was ever an inspiration and delight to me and my world is both dimmed and lighted by constant thought of her."

From around the world, the letters and telegrams poured in, from friends and from those who knew Ruth only across the footlights but felt a sense of personal loss and a compulsion to express it. A light had burned out, and they were not to be consoled.

Isabella Massey was with Salvemini "when the shock came and turned him ice-cold. For two days he was unable to speak of it. Only on the third, when Marion Rawson's letter came, putting our grief into words with such delicacy of sympathy, did he pass it on to me and then we could speak." Salvemini wrote, later, to Neville Rogers: "How true that Ruth had a unifying influence among her friends. Now we are all, all smitten by a great sorrow. I must think of her as she was a few months ago, full of life, joy and goodness."

True to her enduring concern for others, Ruth took great care over her estate. She wrote an extraordinary will in January 1954, carefully reasoned, fairly and equitably distributing, across twenty-three members of her family, amounts precisely judged in accordance with generation. Similar perception was shown in bequests to fifty-three friends at home and abroad. She must have thought and considered long hours to arrive at such widespread benevolence. No one was overlooked. No one expected it. In every case, it made a difference.

The Islesboro property was left to Alice (her executor), for her and two generations of nephews and nieces to enjoy for two years with all expenses, taxes, insurance, and maintenance paid from her estate; when sold, the proceeds would become part of her residuary estate. As her three eldest siblings had predeceased her, leaving no children, Ruth divided her residuary estate into four parts—one part each to Dorothea, Alice, and George and one part equally divided between her brother Paul's living heirs, Paul Draper and Smudge's daughter, Anne Draper.

There were bequests to two officials of Brown Shipley and Company, who had handled her financial affairs for many years, and three hundred pounds to be distributed among the clerks who had assisted, "not forgetting 'Stumpy'" the one-armed doorman at 123 Pall Mall, "to whom I always sent a Christmas gift." Bequests of a hundred pounds each went to The Actor's Benevolent Fund, the Musicians' Benevolent Fund, and, in memory of her nephew Smudge, to the RAF Benevolent Fund.

Ruth made specific bequests to members of the de Bosis and Vivante families, to the widow and sons of Renzo Rendi, and to the daughter of Mario Vinciguerra, Lauro's imprisoned colleagues, as well as a thousand dollars to Salvemini.

In addition, Ruth asked Alice to send a personal remembrance from her possessions to forty-seven friends at home and thirty-two in England and Italy—including Sheila Connolly, who as a child had tended Smudge's grave. Ruth apologized for leaving this task to her sister.

In all, she left a total of about $285,000 in specific bequests. But she also left a legacy to everyone who ever knew or saw her, of intangible uncountable wealth.

Who was Ruth Draper? She was Magic. . . .

Appendix

Glossary of Names

Index

Appendix: The Craft of Ruth Draper

There was such size and style about her work—her touch was absolutely sure.

—Joyce Grenfell, in letters to D. W., 1975

WITH ONLY TWO EXCEPTIONS (*In County Kerry* and *The Return*), none of Ruth Draper's dramatic sketches was based on an actual, specific incident, and never did she put anyone she knew or had seen into a sketch. No characters were mimicked as individuals but represented her distillation of types that she had observed. Her eye and ear and mind were extraordinarily active, registering impressions into her subconscious that later were drawn on to round out and give reality to a sketch that she had conceived; she created—she did not imitate—and each character was an original conception, however influenced by the contents of the vast storehouse of her subconscious memory.

Of the probably sixty sketches that Ruth Draper performed at various times in her long career of forty-seven years (1910–56), thirty-six remained in the repertoire during her last decades; these include four—the most enduring—performed before 1913. Five more came onstage before 1920, including *The Actress* and *Vive la France*, both masterpieces of their kind. The period 1920–29 was her most productive: seventeen new sketches that remained in her repertoire with ten of these being substantial works. After 1929 she wrote only one more of like quality, *Vive la France—1940*, an almost reflexive reaction to the war, in terms of her *Vive la France—1916*. She often played them in tandem.

Very early her work began to show a pattern of development: The *characterizations* became increasingly specific, with descriptive detail building a visual image as well as conveying to the audience a sense of who they were, what they were like, and why they were there. At once they were established in time and place.

The *people whom she evoked* and with whom she played out the scene were established visually and as to their purpose in the scene. Clearly, for her, they existed in space; they were addressed and moved as her eye contact indicated. However imaginary, they had, for her, a physical presence; therefore the audience accepted their reality and saw them, too. She clearly knew what the evoked characters were saying, and the conversations and situations were carefully constructed.

The *imaginary scene* was established quickly: The walls and doors and furniture or other objects were indicated, their purpose known; all remained in place, being neither ignored nor carelessly shifted as the action progressed. Ruth Draper and her imaginary people entered and exited at their appointed place.

Innately, she was a great mime. Functionally, it all worked. There were no loose ends, nothing left floating.

This sense of scene was constantly practiced in her letters. For example, she wrote in 1934: "I'm sitting up in bed—old scene—coverlet covered with letters, telegrams, invitations, papers, monologues. . . . My room is full of flowers from people I don't know. It's a lovely sunny day, the surf is roaring and a warm wind blowing thro' my room and I'm sitting up in a little yellow flowered chiffon 'peignoir,' with heavenly roses, larkspur, lilies, a plant of blue hydrangea near me, the sea sparkling outside—a bunch of lichees near, delicious fruit they are." Noting the importance of color, Ruth saw her imaginary scenes with the same detail and clarity.

Very early, too, a pattern of selection began to emerge in those substantive, enduring character sketches that gradually became, to some degree, short plays: *The Cliffords, Three Generations, Three Breakfasts,* even *The English House Party,* which might well have been carried further as a drama.

Ruth Draper selected a character that she understood and that she felt she could portray, possibly a character in some way part of herself—particularly those socially familiar—or for whom she had sympathy, even empathy. Then she placed that character in a vulnerable situation or at some disadvantage—in conflict with another or with conditions (conditions not necessarily serious, perhaps just a bad day), thus revealing themselves by their reactions.

Ruth Draper had a highly developed sense of the ridiculous, rather than wit or humor, and used it with increasing skill in the juxtaposition of a character with ridiculous situations or remarks in conversation.

In her imaginary telephone conversations, she saw the person on the other end of the wire, and there would be a subtle change in her voice in addressing this unseen but importantly contributing person. Social types and characterizations were so specific that one could believe that Mrs. Clifford and the lady of *The Italian Lesson* may have known one another and that the "Maude" whose telephone call interrupted *The Italian Lesson* could have been Mrs. Mallory. In all of this, Ruth Draper's amazingly detailed and perceptive observation of the way people looked, reacted, and talked was fully exercised.

No matter how slight some of the early characters may have been, they were saved from being "just sketches" by the fact that Ruth Draper was herself moved, even by the silly people she portrayed. She seemed to love and pity them all.

Ruth Draper does not comment—as a writer—on any of her characters. She simply presents a well-observed person in a reasonable, believable situation and leaves judgment to her audience. In the characters of other nationalities—certainly the more substantive ones—one perceives also the national characteristics. She learned to play one character off against another, as in *The Cliffords, The Church in Italy, Three Generations,* and supremely well in *The English House Party.*

Although her monologues remained fluid and lively, the structure did not vary and always went from A to B to C to D, though in performance she might interject a spontaneous remark or piece of business. Not until the last five years or so did she become really consistent, and it was then that she had a stenographer record a number of monologues. They did not read well; much of the text was in the mime and in the actress and her portrayal. As Ruth Draper learned her craft over the years, she occasionally went back over earlier monologues to bring them not up-to-date but more nearly up to her standard as it became more practiced and sophisticated. She never considered "modernizing" a sketch but left it as a "period piece," which, assuredly, it remained.

Ruth Draper's monologues developed a musical structure, almost a melody. With her obvious interest in the sound of words and language, as well as the rhythm and cadence of speech, she developed a pattern of melody in the monologues: pianissimo, fortissimo, crescendo, sostenuto. Most notably, *The Italian Lesson* and *In a Church in Italy*, with changes in language, pace, and rhythm, surely were influenced by her long background in music appreciation and used the full range of her talent and craft. She did not, herself, sing or play any musical instrument; her monologues were the only expression of her musical sense.

Ruth Draper's choice of props and various bits of costuming was perceptive, specific, and carefully calculated to strengthen the image she wished to portray. No other choice would have done so well—the handkerchief, so active a prop in *The Children's Party*, and the very proper, conservative hat, vaguely military, to which she added two long rigid feathers, somehow making it harder, less the Philadelphia lady, to wear as Mrs. Grimmer in *Doctors and Diets*. In each case, it added considerably to the definition of the wearer.

To a fine point, Ruth Draper knew how well she performed. Coming offstage one night, she whipped by her stage manager, saying, "My! I was good—wasn't I?" To a friend who wrote another time of her enjoyment, Ruth replied: "I did not 'feel' I was very good that day. I was not much inspired by the audience—had I known you were in it I should have done better, I know."

Totally professional, Ruth Draper was at the same time the quintessential amateur of her art—the amateur raised to the highest level. She had no knowledge of the technical end of a stage presentation, as witness her appreciation of Lugné-Poe's technique in his staging of *At the Court of Philip IV*, his attention to lighting and sound, to the overall stage effect. When Charles Bowden became Ruth Draper's manager in 1941, lighting cues were nonexistent, but Bowden suggested, as time went on, a few scenes where the lighting could be adjusted to enhance the dramatic effect. Ruth was delighted: "That is wonderful. Now, what else can we do?"

The monologue is one of the most exacting forms of entertainment. In speaking of her own work, Ruth Draper said: "For the young actress I don't think it is a form of acting which should be encouraged because it can't be anything but slightly embarrassing if a person does it with too much effort. It has to be a natural gift. A great many people try to do what I do but are always looking for material that others write for them. I believe in my form of acting doing one's own creations is very important. I've never been able to do anything I myself haven't written."

And then, there is one essential quality: "I have had very good health and great vitality which I think is the most important gift that any artist can have."

In all of Ruth Draper's work, the one irreplaceable element was Ruth Draper herself. Many of the monologues continue to be valid today; some are treasured "period pieces" and should be so regarded. Ruth Draper presented the indestructible core of humanity, the distilled essence of type.

Glossary of Names

Henry Adams (1838–1918). American author (*The Education of Henry Adams*), historian to whom, from 1913 to 1918, Aileen Tone was "niece-in-residence."

Janetta Alexander. A responsible, active member of society.

P. T. Barnum (1810–91). Founder and producer of the great American circus.

Charles C. Burlingham (1858–1959). International lawyer.

Thelma Cazalet-Keir. Member of Parliament from 1931 to 1945. Governor of the British Broadcasting Company (BBC) from 1956 to 1961. Commander of the Order of the British Empire (CBE). Civic responsibilities in education and women's rights.

John Jay Chapman (1862–1933). American writer.

Lady Diana Cooper (1892–1986). A delightful, eccentric, and very beautiful figure in English social, parliamentary, and diplomatic circles from before World War I. Married to Duff Cooper, diplomat, historian, author, and British ambassador to France from 1944 to 1947.

Benedetto Croce (1866–1952). Italian philosopher, historian, critic. Staunch opponent of Fascism. Lived in retirement until 1943, when he became leader of the liberal party.

Marie Curtis (nee **Marie Harjes**). Briefly engaged to Lauro in 1926. With her husband, she stood by Lauro in Paris during this difficult period.

Norman Douglas (1868–1952). English novelist and essayist.

Mildred Dunnock (1900–1991). Noted American actress.

Eleanora Duse (1859–1924). Italian. Widely regarded as a great actress.

Wolcott Gibbs (b. 1902). Editorial writer and drama critic for *The New Yorker*.

Yvette Guilbert (1865–1944). French actress and music hall singer.

Malvina Hoffman (1885–1966). Student of Rodin, became an outstanding sculptor; commissioned by the Field Museum in Chicago to tour around the world, completing nearly one hundred sculptures for a series entitled *The Races of Man*.

Anne Holmes. Daughter of Sir Edmund and Lady Phipps. Close family friend.

Henry James (1843–1916). American novelist living mainly in London and Rye, Sussex. Became a British subject in 1915. Awarded the Order of Merit by King George V.

Jenny Lind (1820–87). Noted Swedish soprano.

Nancy Cox MacCormack. American sculptor and friend to Lillian de Bosis.

Giacomo Matteotti (1885–1924). During his third term in the Chamber of Deputies, Matteotti denounced the fraud of recent elections. Ten dates later, walking to the Chamber, Matteotti was abducted and murdered.

Guisseppi Mazzini (1805–1872). Outstanding Italian patriot and revolutionary, working untiringly and effectively in exile toward the Risorgimento.

J. P. Morgan (1837–1913). American. Widely influential international banker.

Margaret Oliphant (1828–97). Victorian writer of now well-forgotten novels, including *The Chronicles of Carlingford*.

Ignace Jan Paderewski (1860–1941). Polish. Composer, pianist, statesman.

General John J. Pershing (1860–948). Distinguished commander of American forces in France during World War I.

Matilda Pfeiffer. Italian living in Cambridge, Massachusetts, as wife of an MIT professor. Senior and wise friend to Lauro.

Cole Porter (1891–1964). Yale '13. Composer of many Broadway hits. In 1917, during World War I, enlisted in French Foreign Legion, transferring to the French army in 1919.

Mrs. Harold Pratt. Social and civic leader in New York.

Mrs. Whitelaw Reid. Wife of owner of *The New York Tribune*. Influential, responsible, civic-minded.

Max Reinhardt (1873–1943). Austrian stage director and impresario in the German-speaking theatre. Produced *Everyman* in Salzburg, a great center of summer music festivals.

Elizabeth Robins (1872–1943). American actress holding stage rights to many Ibsen plays, which she performed on the English stage. Henrick Ibsen (1828–1906) was a Norwegian playwright; many of his plays and characters have become classics of the English stage.

Corinne Robinson (later **Corinne Alsop**). Very active in state civic and political affairs. Mother of Joseph Alsop Jr., Stewart, John, and Corinne.

Neville Rogers (d. 1986). English literature professor; editor of special edition of Shelley.

Elihu Root (1845–1937). American lawyer, statesman; served in two presidential cabinets. Nobel Peace Prize 1912. Instrumental in the founding of the United Nations and the World Court of International Justice.

Rosselli brothers (Carlo and Nello). Active anti-Fascists. Murdered in France by Italian agents in July 1937.

Bertrand Russell (later **Third Earl Russell**) (1872–1970). Philosopher, author, and distinguished mathematician.

Gaetano Salvemini. Italian historian and anti-Fascist activist.

John Singer Sargent (1850–1925). American painter, known mainly for portraits, who worked in Paris and London.

Ned Sheldon. Playwright.

Ellen Terry (1847–1928). Legendary actress who starred on the English stage with Henry Irving. In 1931 published her delightful correspondence with George Bernard Shaw. Great admirer of Ruth Draper and her work.

Mrs. Yates Thompson. Eldest daughter of George Smith, founder of the *Dictionary of National Biography* and publisher and friend to many notable writers of the time.

Anthony Trollope (1815–1882). Prolific Victorian novelist whose Barsetshire novels remain popular today.

Carl Van Vechten (1880–1966). American music critic of *The New York Times*, writer of music, supporter of Negro cultural interests. Married Fania Marinoff, Russian actress. Friend and editor to Gertrude Stein.

Edith Wharton (1862–1937). American novelist and intellectual whose stories, some of which have been made into films, are popular today. Lived many years in France.

Oscar Wilde (1854–1901). Irish writer of witty plays, including *The Importance of Being Earnest*, and the long poem *The Ballad of Reading Gaol*. Jailed for two years at hard labor on a charge of homosexuality. Died in Dieppe, leaving a wife and two sons.

Lucy Ann Whitaker. Friend who cared for Paul and Smudge Draper as small boys.

Arnold Whitridge (1891–1989). Educator, author. Served in the British army from 1914 to 1917 and in the U.S. Army from 1917 to 1919. Colonel in Ninth U.S. Air Force during World War II in combat intelligence. Master of Calhoun College, Yale University, from 1932 to 1942. Grandson of Matthew Arnold, English poet and writer. Great grandson of Dr. Arnold of Rugby.

Alexander Woollcott (1887–1948). Drama critic for *The New Yorker*.

Index

Index

Index

Index

Index

musical structure, of monologues, 125
Mussolini, Benito, 65, 66, 70, 73
Mylnarski, Aniela, 79

naivete, 81
Neighborhood Playhouse, 32
nephews and nieces, 96–97, 120; at Isles-
boro, 98–100, 113
Nevile, Thomas, 114–15
New Yorker (magazine), 6
New York Herald Tribune, 54
New York Sun, 11, 12
New York Times, 14, 43, 72, 93
New York University, 91
Niall, Mahlon, 6
Nitti, Francesco, 67
North American Student Movement, 40

obituary, 118
Ocampo, Victoria, 87
Opening a Bazaar, 1, 3, 114
Osler, Sir William, 14
Oving (Thompson home), 105

Paderewski, Ignacy Jan, 14, 19, 21
Paris, 19, 52–53; post–World War II, 111;
World War I and, 35–36
Peat, Harold R., 89, 116
performance: beginnings of, 21, 22; first
stage, 32; hypnotic quality of, 4; Lon-
don debut, 46–48; for Mussolini, 56–
57; presence onstage, 7; professionalism
in, 53; self-awareness in, 6
Perkins, Elizabeth, 32, 63
Pershing, John J., 37, 40, 44
personality, 7–8, 98; Puritan qualities in,
10–11
Pfeiffer, Matilda, 65, 67, 74
Phipps, Jessie (Mrs. William Walton), 19,
44, 48, 106–7
Phipps, John C., 118, 119
Phipps, Nora Astor and Phyllis, 107
Phipps, Paul, 44, 107
Pickman, Esther, 65
Playbill, 4
poetry, 60–61, 99
Pratt, Mrs. Harold, 22, 33, 35
prejudice, against theatre, 31

Presbitero, Marchesa Katherine, 57, 58
Puritan qualities, 10–11

Queen Elizabeth (ship), 109, 112
Queen Mary (ship), 113

Rain (Maugham), 50
Rawson, Marion Enthoven, 102, 119, 120
Reavis, Wilhelmina, 115
recitations, at parties, 25
Red Cross, 36, 37, 45; charity benefits for,
33, 34, 87; Martha Draper's work for,
43–44
Reid, Mrs. Whitelaw, 35
Reinhardt, Max, 56
Rendi, Renzo, 66, 78, 111, 120
reviews and critiques, 47–48, 96
Richardson, Anne and George, 49–50
ridiculous, sense of, 124
Risorgimento, 65, 79
Robins, Elizabeth, 106
Robinson, Corinne. *See* Alsop, Corinne
Robinson
Rogers, Neville, 26, 56, 63–64, 74, 119,
120
role playing, childhood, 12, 13
romance: with de Bosis, 57–62, 63–64, 79–
80; vs. freedom, 55–56
Rome, 18; performance in, 56–57
Roosevelt, Eleanor, 90, 92
Roosevelt, Franklin D., 92
Roosevelt, Kermit, 17
Roosevelt, Mrs. James, 22
Roosevelt, Theodore, 17
Rosselli, Carlo, 101, 102, 111, 114
Rosselli, Maria, 114
Rosselli, Nello, 101, 114
Rubinstein, Arthur, 51, 58, 62, 79, 87, 117;
evenings at Edith Grove and, 23, 24, 49
Rubinstein, Eva, 117
Russell, Bertrand and Alys, 101
Ruth Draper Benevolent Fund, 86

Salmond, Felix, 23, 24, 87, 98
Salmond, Helen, 24, 87, 107
Salvadori, Massimo, 80
Salvemini, Gaetano, 69, 106, 113, 114, 120;
anti-Fascism and, 64, 78, 101–2; de Bosis

Index

Dorothy Warren, a fifth-generation New Yorker, graduated from Miss Spence's School in 1925 and grew up with many associations in Ruth Draper's world. Always active in various charitable projects, Miss Warren spent many years as a business executive. Now retired, she devotes her energies to photography and biography.